MW01593819

ONE WORLD
ONE HEART

Let Peace Begin with Me

Marilyn Mills

ONE WORLD ONE HEART

Let Peace Begin with Me

Copyright © 2019 by Marilyn Mills

All rights reserved. No part of this book may be reproduced or transmitted in any form or by any means, electronic or mechanical, including photocopying, recording, or by any information storage and retrieval system without the written permission of the author, except where permitted by law.

ISBN: 9781089325130

We shine our light

And discover gifts unknown

We listen to the messenger

Recalibrating our thoughts and words

We reach out to others

And love our children

Showing them the way

Nurturing friendships

And giving and receiving without limits

Forgiving ourselves

We find our peace

And sharing our love

We heal the world and ourselves in the cosmic dance called life.

MSM

DEDICATION

My brother Gary was the funny one in our family. He could find the humor in almost anything—and usually did. In his forties he decided to write down his childhood memories for posterity. From the nuns at St. Mary's parochial school to working and playing on the farm, he had a great recollection of past events. Because inspiration can strike at any time, he would carry sticky notes in his wallet, and if he remembered something good, he would jot a few lines to be added to the story later.

When he decided to share them with us, we discovered he had a real flair for storytelling. His writing was insightful and often humorous. Through his stories, he captured the heart and soul of those long-ago memories. While reading them, I realized his childhood was vastly different than mine for many reasons; being a boy, born eight years earlier, and his birth order—being one of the oldest in a large family versus being one of the youngest.

An unassuming guy, he never believed writing was one of his gifts, yet it clearly was *one of his gifts.*

While working on our beloved farm, he was killed in a tragic accident in May 2019. Everyone—his wife, daughter, family, and friends were devastated at the loss. We know his spirit lives on, but we will always miss his presence, his humor, and the essence that made him special.

It is with love and affection that I dedicate this book to him. Here is an excerpt from one of his stories when he was a Boy Scout.

We had a series of what we called survival campouts, although the level of survival skills fell well short of pioneering standards. We camped at the end of the two- track road in Oscar Sundell's woods, which was the old ice road from Stony Lake. Our pup tents were pitched under the big maple tree (now dead and gone) at the road's end. We then started surviving as best we knew how.

Our leaders had to pick the right time or else we had no chance. Our food had to be in season, you see. Wild strawberries were picked, an activity which will, in of and by itself, work up an appetite. They were so puny that it seemed an eternity to pick enough to matter. We picked wintergreen leaves to steep in hot water to make tea. Very weak, I thought. We had bows and arrows and a rifle— I hope it was only a BB gun—and a dipping net and started to hunt frogs. There weren't that many around so we did what any resourceful pioneer would do—hop in the back of Paul Schmideknecht's pick up and have him drive us to a better source. Our first stop was a roadside ditch near Dan Schiller's. There were some frogs there but also some leeches. That was the end of that, and Paul took us to Flower Creek. We waded down the creek sowing destruction in our wake. We caught an astounding number of frogs, maybe 80 to 100. One quick cut with a knife and the frogs were liberated from their legs. Paulie was the bag holder for our patrol, using some sort of a leather satchel but Joe Jonseck of the Crow patrol just stuffed them into his pocket. Well, his pocket had a hole and most of them were lost so we had to share. Grilled over a campfire, they tasted very good, like chicken.

We found a snapping turtle on the road and Big Paul (Paulie's dad) converted it into soup. He was a most handy guy to have around when living off the land. He would have made a great boy scout. He had a lot of woodsy and craftsy knowledge. Another time—this was a different campout—we were in such dire straits that Gary Jonseck and Marty Keeler swiped some asparagus from Evard's patch. Yes, I ate it.

Table of Contents

Chapter 1: Your Light

When we lift the veil we see
The message was and always will be *love*

I don't know if anyone ever told you, but your light is something special. Science tells us every living thing is emitting electromagnetic radiation or energy. I grew up in Michigan and I make the trek back every summer to see my family. In the summer months, Michigan is buzzing with activities and people are outside from morning till night, enjoying the great weather. When I'm there, I like to go for walks in the evening and I always stop in amazement when I catch my first glimpse of fireflies. They cluster in large groups and once it's completely dark, thousands of them appear as tiny blinking lights, letting the world know they exist. In a way, we're also like that. We're here living our lives every day, but no one sees our true beauty until *we shine our light*.

All of us come here with two deeply embedded innate desires: *to be our true, authentic, spiritual selves and to be*

7

loved truly and deeply. Sometimes we forget we have a light within. We forget we are Spirits, here to grow and love as we experience life. And the most important thing we sometimes forget? *Love solves everything.* When we have peace in our hearts and kindness in our voices, we are creating a climate of acceptance that is deeply affecting others in a positive way. When we share our smile, friendliness, and acceptance of others, we are strengthening those aspects of ourselves and these actions demonstrate to everyone that we are choosing love over fear. In those moments, we are a powerful reminder that all of us come with gifts to share. Do you wonder what your gifts might be? That is a question worth asking and exploring.

In life, sometimes we're the student and other times we're the teacher. We serve as a teacher when we reach out to help, guide, and encourage someone. When we connect with the conscious intention of giving love and acceptance to others, we're having a profound effect on those people, the world, and ourselves. Thoughts and actions rooted in love have a good vibration that is emanating out into the world, touching everyone. In fact, the positive energy you're giving off is leaving a lasting imprint on everything it touches. You are more powerful than you know.

All of us are awakening to the fact that our love has potency, and we can plant the seeds of our love a thousand different ways in the spaces that make up our lives. These opportunities will often come and go quickly. Will you take a few minutes to chat with your lonely neighbor or help someone across the street? Would you give someone a quarter if they were standing by a meter, looking for change in their pockets? A stranger did this once for me, never saying a word. His gift of 25 cents most certainly saved me from a thirty-dollar parking ticket that afternoon in San Francisco.

Any time we take a moment to say hello or show kindness, we are restoring people's faith in humanity. A random act of kindness that takes thirty seconds may be the one thing that makes someone smile today. Any kindness, big or small, has love and connection embedded in it. Connection is meaningful because whenever we reach out, we are bridging the gulf of separateness and isolation that many people are feeling today. Because nothing in the world happens in a vacuum, our actions may inspire others to step out of their comfort zone to connect with someone. So many positive things are happening simultaneously in these moments, including putting us in the mindset of our natural state: love. In the end, love is all there is.

What Comes Around Goes Around

On one of my trips home to visit my mom, I volunteered to give up my seat on an overbooked flight out of San Francisco. I sat at the gate and watched everyone board as I waited to discover my fate. Would I be hanging around SFO another four hours or boarding the aircraft? Five minutes before the plane was to disembark, the agent, a lovely African-American woman, called me up and said, "Thanks, but we won't need you, but give me a minute here." She continued to work on her computer, and I stood there for seemingly forever, wondering, What is taking so long? A few minutes later she handed me my boarding pass. When I looked down and saw my seat number was 2A, I realized she had seated me in first class. Instead of being crammed into a coach seat for the next four hours to Chicago, I was going to sit in a large, comfortable leather seat, be served any beverage of my choice throughout the flight, and have a hot breakfast served on a china plate with real silverware. What a way to start my vacation! This lovely, thoughtful woman reminded me that we all have the power to make someone's day with a kind gesture. Some people would call my offer to give up my seat and her reciprocating gift instant karma.

Serendipity Far from Home

I love traveling, and I've had some memorable experiences on my journeys. One of my big trips was to Europe when I was twenty-seven. After reading, in fourth grade, about the obliteration of Pompeii by Mount Vesuvius, I quietly decided that someday I would visit those archeological ruins. As I learned about the Renaissance and European history, I kept adding new places to my bucket list: Versailles and the Hall of Mirrors, the London Tower where Henry the VIII famously beheaded his wife, Anne Boleyn, the ceiling of the Sistine chapel, the statue of David and the Pieta, the British museum, the Louvre, and more. After college, I began saving money, and two years later, I was on my first international trip to Europe for six weeks of backpacking. I flew into London to spend five days, and then my plan was to travel to Paris. Once in London, I bought a one-way ticket there and didn't think much about the arrival time: 7:30 p.m. It was late October, and by 6:30 p.m., it was dark outside.

While on that forty-five-minute flight to Paris, I had the good fortune to sit next to a young woman named Emilie. Her English was excellent, and we began chatting. She told me she lived in Paris, and I began telling her about my trip and what countries I planned to visit while in Europe. The conversation was easy, and she gushed that she had recently visited New York City and how much she loved it. New York and the people there had made a big impression on her. She asked where I was staying in Paris and I told her I didn't know. I had planned to use my guidebook to find a hostel. She looked concerned and said, "Let me help you find a place once we land." I remember leaving the airport with her and taking a subway into a neighborhood. We then walked to a small hotel on a quiet street. She did all the talking to the clerk and I'm sure she informed him of my situation. (An American backpacker who speaks very little French) Then she turned to me and said, "Here is your key. Breakfast is included and there is the dining room." She pointed to a room across the lobby. Then she gave me her phone number and said, "If you have any problems, call me. Call me anyway, and we can meet for dinner before you leave Paris."

We did have dinner a few nights later; she and her boyfriend took me to a great local café. It was charming and filled with Parisians. I remember it looked like a scene out of a movie. The backdrop: a crisp fall evening, the location: a neighborhood bistro with warm ambient lighting filled with fresh faced people chattering away in French. As I sat across from them, drinking wine and eating dinner, I marveled at my good fortune and how life is filled with so many unexpected surprises. I was beginning to realize that in life, magic happens when we step outside our comfort zone and trust in Spirit. I would have been too intimidated to go there on my own, so I felt very lucky to have met Emilie. Although I was a stranger, this warm-hearted couple treated me like a long, lost friend. I asked her that night why she had gone so far out of her way to help me. She said, "When I was in New York everyone was so nice to me. I wanted you to have the same experience in Paris." Emilie's kindness is what stands out in my memory when I remember my 'chance encounter' with her and my time in Paris.

Universal Laws and Creating our Life Experiences
The Law of Cause and Effect says our thoughts, behaviors, and actions create specific consequences that manifest and create our life as we experience it. Doesn't it

seem possible that if we are loving and kind, we will get those experiences back from others? We create a chain of events by thinking about something, positive or negative, and then taking action. Those events then play out and have a reverberating effect that impacts others and us, sometimes for years to come.

Emilie made a decision that night to help me. She was in London and on her way home. She easily could have said good luck and been on her way. That's what 99% of people would have done. Instead, she helped a fellow traveler and made a powerful impression on me; so much that I am retelling her story thirty years later. Her kindness and that of many others since then has made me keenly aware of the positive effect that helping has on others and it's shaped me into someone who wants to give back. That is the ripple effect of positive thoughts and actions, and it's real. We are creating our experiences every day, whether we realize it or not. From the moment we wake up till we fall asleep, our actions (which are a manifestation of our thoughts), are having a profound effect on others, just as their actions are affecting us. That is the symbiotic relationship we have with every person here on the planet; the invisible thread connecting us to everyone else.

The Law of Attraction says we attract to ourselves whatever we think about—good or bad. Author Jack Canfield says, "The Law of Attraction is the most powerful law in the universe; whatever you focus on and give your attention to will come back to you." The energy we are giving off becomes very important in creating our experiences now and in our future. If we want to attract positive people and experiences into our lives, we must give off that same vibration. Part of our spiritual awakening is realizing we have the power to create anything we want. What do you want to create and manifest in your life? I like to imagine a world filled with kind and generous people who are living together in harmony. When I travel, I always imagine I will meet great people, all will be well, and the trip will be easy and effortless. *It always is.*

Oprah and The Law of Attraction

Larry King interviewed Oprah many years ago on his television show and she told a wonderful story about seeing the movie, *The Secret, The Law of Attraction*, and reading the book, *The Color Purple*. She says, "I became obsessed with this story. I ate, slept, and thought all the time about *The Color Purple*." She moved to Chicago and got a call from a casting agent, asking if she would like to come and audition for a movie. She had never gotten a call in her life from anyone for a movie. She asked if it was for *The Color Purple* and they said, "No, it's for a movie called *Moon Song*." She told them, "I've been praying for *The Color Purple*." She went to the audition and found out it *was* for *The Color Purple*.

Months went by and she didn't hear anything. She began to believe she didn't get the call back because she was fat. She went to a fat farm and she was praying and crying about the part of Sophia in the movie. She wanted it so badly. While she was there, she received a phone call from Steven Spielberg, who was directing and producing *The Color Purple*. He was calling to invite her to California to discuss the part. Oprah says, "That moment absolutely changed my life forever. I had drawn *The Color Purple* into my life. I didn't know Steven Spielberg or Quincy Jones. It changed the way I thought about my life."

Bright Lights

We are lucky because there are many beautiful people (souls) among us like Emilie, who are shining their light and sharing their beautiful spirit. I call these people **bright lights**. They are kind and loving; they are the peacemakers of the world. They choose to see the cup half full in life and they act with love and compassion without fail. We are drawn to them and trust them because they emanate goodness. They are walking their path with awareness that we are all spirits here on a journey to discover and develop our soul's greatness. This is why they can forgive other's mistakes and move on—there is no need to hold a grudge. They see the beauty in everyone, even those who don't yet have a bright light. *They uplift us with their positive energy and show us the world is better when we hold love and peace in our hearts.* Do you know someone who is a bright light? I have known many, and this is what gives me hope for our future.

You may be a bright light, which is why you are drawn to this book. You know this in your heart because your intuition tells you it's true. Or, you are on the brink of discovering this—you are in the metamorphosis stage of becoming a bright light. I welcome you to join me in using our thoughts to create a better world with more peace and love—for everyone. It's time for us to discover our spiritual destiny. We're on this journey together.

A New Way of Thinking

As we shift into this spiritual awakening, we become increasingly aware of our divinity and purpose. We don't want to just exist; we want to develop our gifts and make a difference in the world. Sometimes though, we unknowingly sabotage ourselves with thoughts that separate us from others and from Spirit. We want to let go of our limiting thoughts so we can expand our beliefs and actions to create a higher spiritual vibration.

First, we let go of the belief that we are separate from others; we are not. **We are all one**. To help integrate this into your thoughts, this can be a mantra you say every day whenever you think about it: "We are all one." This belief that we're separate from each other has been taught since we were young, but it's simply not true. It's important to integrate this belief into your thoughts, because this truth is opening your mind to Spirit and all that is possible. Once our limited thinking is released, our ability to create becomes unlimited.

Second, we understand when we hurt someone; we hurt ourselves because there is a beautiful, mysterious, intangible thread that connects ALL souls to each other. We're not only connected to our family members and friends—but everyone, including the strangers you pass on the street, the neighbors you haven't met yet, and everyone else across the globe. We are all children of God and *we are all one.*

Lastly, we begin to recognize and let go of thoughts not based in love. As we awaken and begin living consciously, we acknowledge the tremendous power we wield with our thoughts and words. If we catch ourselves feeling negativity towards someone, (racism, resentment, anger, judgment) recognizing it is the first step to changing it. We can say, "I choose to release those negative thoughts, because they're hurting me and the other person." We *can* consciously choose our thoughts. If you can't send positive thoughts to others yet, then choose to be calm and neutral when thinking about them. This action could be directed towards one person (sibling, parent, coworker, ex-spouse, or a group of people) You are recalibrating the way you think, and as long as you are moving in the direction of love, you're doing a great job. When we are learning something new, every time we practice, it gets easier and feels more natural. What's the end result of releasing negative thoughts? We feel lighter and happier as we emanate love and peace. Great effort always brings great rewards.

We begin our path of awakened consciousness knowing that:

- We have a beautiful, divine light within that guides us.
- On a soul level, that spark of divinity (our light within) is linking us to one another.
- Our thoughts have the power to *heal the world and ourselves* because we are all connected.
- Miracles are created through love, not magic.

In one of my favorite movies, *The Wizard of Oz*, Dorothy asks Glinda the Good Witch how she should begin her journey to Oz. Glinda replies, "It's always best to start at the beginning." We start healing the world by *reaching out with love* to family, friends, neighbors, acquaintances, and strangers. We will positively affect everyone here, because our love is powerful, we're all connected on a soul level, and millions of us are ready to embrace this message.

Let your light shine.

Chapter 2: Your Gifts

Have you ever wondered, "Why am I here—what is my life's purpose?" There have been times in my life when I've wondered to myself, *Am I here to take up space or is there a reason why I was born?*

We all come here with gifts to share and discovering them is a personal journey each of us must take. The process of learning about ourselves begins as small children and continues until the day we die. Discovering who we are, what we love, and what we came to share should be one of the most important goals in our lives. Many of us are completely unaware of our gifts, probably because we haven't thought about it much. It's akin to going down the rabbit hole in *Alice in Wonderland*. What will you find hidden within that you never knew existed? We take this journey of self-discovery to mine the beauty of our soul; it's that drop of divinity within us that inspires and compels us to shine our light.

What is your soul's purpose? What do you want to do, to be, or to accomplish during this lifetime? Discovering your purpose starts with looking inside yourself and being honestly introspective. Uncover what makes you appreciate the gift of life and inspires you to be your best. We all come here with multiple missions, that on a soul level, we chose long before our birth.

Maybe you came here to be a comedian, to help people laugh and take away their stress. Comedians are modern day jesters, and they offer a great gift to the rest of us. Laughing is one of the best things we can do to de-stress, and too often, we forget to laugh, play, and enjoy life because we get so busy with work and other obligations. Children are great to be around because they help us remember that life doesn't have to be so serious. Having fun and enjoying life is so important, because *one of our missions is to be happy*, and we all love being around happy people and their uplifting energy.

Messages from Spirit

Spirit is always whispering, guiding, and giving us clues about our missions. Have you heard any messages lately? Many people pray and meditate to open up the channel of communication with Spirit. Messages can come in many forms; conversations with friends or strangers, a thought that spontaneously pops into our heads while we're driving, taking a walk, or upon awakening in the morning. We may dream or journal or practice yoga and be given messages from Spirit. They can come at any time or any place. You may suddenly have a very clear thought about something or someone that you didn't have before. That is Spirit guiding you. Pay attention, relax, and receive. The messages come through easiest when we are relaxed and not worried. Now you see why it's a gift to be around people who make us laugh. Having a peaceful, relaxed mind brings us closer to Spirit/God and our own divinity.

We don't have to be passive and wait for guidance to come to us. We can ask God/Spirit for answers to our questions. Praying or meditating, we can ask, "What message do you have for me today?" Or you could be specific, asking, "Is staying in this job or this relationship a good idea?" "Should I go back to school and follow my dreams?" Don't be afraid to ask and know that once you do, an answer is coming. Be patient and let yourself be open to whatever thought or message comes to you. Remember, when we ask a question, the answer can show up any time. When we ask, we will get an answer. It may not be the answer we're hoping for, but instead, be an answer that gives us the peace we are looking for.

There will be obstacles to deal with on our life's journey—our path to self- discovery. Think about Dorothy's journey in *The Wizard of Oz*. As she travels through Oz on her way to the Emerald City, she keeps running into obstacles caused by the wicked witch of the west, but she is also constantly guided and helped by Glinda, the good witch. If Dorothy's story were unfolding on our planet, we would refer to Glinda as her guardian angel or spirit guide. It's a wonderful story because it is metaphor for our own life's journey. Dorothy starts out naïve and inexperienced, but as she travels on (lives her life) she discovers strengths she wasn't aware of and she begins to believe in herself. She repeatedly pushes past her fears, opens her heart, and shows compassion and love to others. It's a journey of self- determination and self-discovery.

Innate Gifts

Natural talents are the gifts we bring in with us on this journey through time and space. As we develop them, they will bring us joy, and when we share them with others, that joy will increase exponentially for everyone. Why?

Because we are meant to share our gifts—it's one of our missions. Think of singers, musicians, writers, actors, scientists, artists, healers, and leaders. They have made our world a better place by sharing their gifts and talents. Musicians and singers listened to their intuition and took classes, along with practicing their instrument or voice for hundreds, if not thousands of hours. Some entertainers work many years honing their craft before getting their big break. They listened to their gut and not to those who said, "You'll never make it." All of them used the Law of Attraction and The Law of Cause and Effect, along with their gifts, to create their life, their way. You don't have to be famous to have many incredible gifts to share. What kind of life are you going to create? What gifts do you want to share?

Several years ago, I was trying to decide if I should go back to college and start a new career. I prayed and thought about it a lot. I read books on changing careers and looked at some master's programs at different universities. I was also asking for guidance on a bigger question, the biggest question of all: "What is my mission in life? Do I have a mission? If I do, why don't I know it? I felt a little lost and wondered, "How could I not know the answer at this point in my life?" This question weighed heavily on my mind and I didn't know if I would ever get the answer. A few months later, it came to me as a crystal clear thought.

Your mission: To be the best version of yourself every day and to help others whenever possible.

One aspect of my mission is to be an "encourager." As an extrovert, I often find myself in conversations with many different people, from good friends to strangers. As we talk and the conversation meanders, they will often share with me what is going on in their lives and their dreams and goals. From strangers on airplanes, to coworkers, friends, and the twenty-year-old guy stringing my tennis racquet, they share their dreams with me, but they also share their fears and doubts related to achieving their goals.

I find myself listening and thinking about what encouraging words I might offer. With life experience, we learn that obstacles are just something to work out as we pursue our dreams. Having someone share how they worked out a problem often will get the other person to see that their road block isn't insurmountable at all. And sometimes, just having someone say, "I see so many benefits to you pursuing your dream of....." is enough to give him or her the incentive to start a new goal or finish the one they're working on.

Nondrinkers are designated drivers in the United States because they can be counted on to keep others safe who are drinking. I've discovered through these conversations I'm working a mission called, "designated cheerleader." I'm here to nudge people in the direction of their goals and dreams. I accept my role, knowing that helping others is part of my mission and there are many people in the world who need someone cheering them on. You may be on my squad and be a designated cheerleader too.

I felt a sense of relief knowing that my career choice, in relation to my mission, didn't really matter; it was having a conscious awareness of my mission that mattered most. The income-earning job we have in life is not necessarily critical to our spiritual journey. That's not to say that you shouldn't pursue any career that calls you to it. Often we are drawn to work that will help us express our true selves and draw on our strengths, so getting clarity on how we can live our lives in a *meaningful way* is what's important. For many of us, it will be service of one kind or another.

I have worked for over fifteen years with children in preschools and school-age programs. I currently teach in a preschool inclusion classroom, and my students range in age from three to five years old. An inclusion classroom is one in which children with special needs are mainstreamed into a general education classroom. Some of my inclusion students have been diagnosed with ASD or Autism Spectrum Disorder. My students are wonderful, and I love being around them. They exude curiosity, kindness, creativity, and joyfulness. When I look at them, I see a purity of spirit, which is beautiful *and* inspiring. One of my missions is to support them in building their self-confidence to believe they can do or be anything in life.

Your mission could be related to your career, your family, a hobby, or an interest you have. Maybe all of the above—let's not rule anything out, because anything is possible. We can have multiple missions in life and handle all of them beautifully.

The Big Question

Until we have peace and happiness within ourselves, it will be difficult to discover and fulfill our missions. We must all come to terms with two things: what will make us happy and what are we passionate about? Very often, they will be one and the same. If you don't know, it's because you are not in touch with your innermost wishes and desires. Many people feel guilty if they pursue a dream, feeling they are being selfish and taking time away from their family. As long as you are a responsible adult, please know that you are not being selfish to pursue happiness. On the contrary, the happier we are the more we can affect those around us, because the positive energy we're giving off is leaving a lasting imprint on everything it touches. If you think about it, happy people are a gift to everyone. When someone walks in smiling, doesn't that make us feel much better than someone who comes in complaining?

When I was in high school, my best friend was a girl named Karin. Her dad was a physician practicing family medicine in the small town close to where I grew up. Her mom was a registered nurse who worked in his office on and off through the years. The time came when her mom, Maythia, wanted more, so in her forties she went back to school to pursue a new career in counseling. We lived in a rural area, so her mom drove quite a distance a few evenings a week for a couple of years. Her family had to step up and help, and Karin would sometimes make dinner and the kids started doing their own laundry.

I was really shocked because at my house we never made dinner or did our own laundry. My mom always did it. Back in 1970s rural Michigan, the idea of your kids cooking and cleaning while you were in college was not the norm, at least among the friends I knew. I saw it was a good thing for everyone in the family. Pursuing her master's degree made her mom feel happy and fulfilled and asking Karin and her siblings to step up and help was teaching them important life skills. Maythia was also sending a powerful message to her children: pursue your dreams and goals, and if it requires sacrifice, the end result will be worth it. Like Karin's mom, pursuing our dreams can bring us fulfillment, and then we can genuinely support others in their dreams—without feeling resentful. When we're happy and living a life of our making, we're shining our light, and others enjoy being around our energy. We need millions of people to find their happiness. Can you visualize what that world will look like? I definitely can.

Your Dreams

They say the number one regret among elderly people is they didn't follow their dreams. So many people look back on their lives and wish they had taken a risk, been less afraid to try new things, and seized opportunities when they were presented. If you are in an unfulfilling relationship or job, think about how long you want to stay there, knowing that in life, time is the one thing you don't get back. Don't waste a moment being unhappy because you feel powerless to make a change. Life is short, and the years will go by fast. As Oscar Wilde said, "No man is rich enough to buy back his past." Think about what you really want and then do something to make it happen. It's not enough to tell our friends and ourselves we want to change. We must take action. Make a phone call or go talk to someone who has information about what you are interested in. Going back to high school or college starts with filling out an application and then registering for classes. Believe in your ability to manifest your dreams and know that the universe will support you.

Visualization is a great tool; use your imagination and see yourself where you want to be. Children are always using their imagination when they play. We have the power of imagination within us too. What really helps is when we visualize *and* talk about our dreams to others and to ourselves. (Words expressed out loud give our goals credibility and a sense of realism) If you want to move to the city, open a business, sing professionally, or go to law school, share your ideas. I am amazed that whenever I talk about my dreams and goals, suddenly someone is offering an idea or information that will help me with that particular goal. When I am thinking about a goal that seems a little "out there" or hard to imagine I could reach, I'll tell myself, "Spirit has a way of making things work out." What is one goal or dream that you want to start working on today? What is one step you could take? Just do it!

Helping Each Other

We want to surround ourselves with good people who we can count as friends, and who know they can also count on us. Choosing positive, caring people to be in our lives becomes very important for our missions to be successful, because we all need encouragement. Often people are afraid to do something new, so they postpone taking action. I know what it's like to feel stuck and unable to move forward; I've been there many times and it's not a good feeling. If you know someone is feeling overwhelmed with getting started on a goal, offering to help can make a huge difference for them. Maybe they need help applying for financial aid for college, or they don't know how to update their resume to make it look presentable. At times, our dreams can be daunting, and we need people to tell us, "You can do it and I'll help you."

It's interesting that when we help others, it has a way of coming back to us in the form of a kindness being returned at another place and time. *What comes around really does go around.* I'm always a bit surprised at how often this boomerang effect happens; I see it all the time in my life and in others' lives too.

Nurturing Children and Their Gifts

I've worked with hundreds of families as a teacher, and if you have raised or are raising a loving and caring child, you are doing a great service and I thank you. We all thank you, because in order to have a happy child who cares about others, you must be a dedicated parent; someone who puts their children first. You must model patience, kindness, and forgiveness. You make a million small sacrifices that few even notice. As a parent, your mission is to *love your children unconditionally*, so they will know in their hearts they are loved, and they deserve to be loved. They will come to believe that love solves everything and hold this as one of their universal truths. Their presence will make the world better just by being here. In the future, when we meet your children as adults, we will see you through them. Your children become your legacy.

Our planet is getting ready for a big shift—one that is going to make it a more spiritually enlightened place. Many of the children and young adults now here are bright lights with a special mission: To help uplift our planet's vibration. You may know a child who is here to help transform the world. I have met many children who I intuitively know are here to help guide our planet to a better place. They have an amazing blend of intellect, emotional maturity, and compassion. They are loving and their light is beautiful. If you see your child possesses a desire to help others, they are manifesting one of their gifts. With love and encouragement from you, they will discover and develop all their innate gifts, which will be a blessing for all of us.

Children are the most important piece of life's puzzle because they are our tomorrow, our great hope for something better. Let's give our children all the love and encouragement they need to bring their gifts to fruition. We owe it to them, our future, and ourselves.

Discovering Our Missions

Do you know what your mission is? No one can answer this for you, but here are some hints. It may be described as one or all of the things below. It will always be positive—we are not here to cause harm to anyone or anything.

- It makes you happy and you are passionate about it.

- It's a gift and you share it. It could be your smile, kindness, and love.

- You serve others or the planet in some way. (I have a friend who advocates for animals every day.)

- You intuitively know it is your mission. It's a pervasive feeling/thought.

Our missions can change as we go through life, because we're continually growing as spiritual beings. All missions are valuable because they help us express our unique gifts. Contrary to how it looks or feels at times, there is no pass or fail in life. There is only progress on our spiritual path. We are all here to love and learn and grow as spiritual beings. That's why being here is such a gift. We all have a capacity for greatness, and when we discover and share our gifts, we fulfill our legacy as we heal the planet. It's perfect.

Being happy and following our dreams is

healing the world.

Chapter 3: The Messenger

Many times, God or Spirit will send someone to help us in our hour of need. Although we are often aware of coincidences or serendipity happening around us, they say there are no coincidences in life. How often have you had someone come up exactly at the right time to help you in some way? I think all of us have experienced it. It's happened so many times in my life, I've lost count. From friends, acquaintances, and even strangers, I have been given advice and help at critical times in my life, all of which have strengthened my faith that there are wonderful people in the world, and *Spirit is always with me*.

Sinking Deep

Depression and suicide have never been easy subjects to talk about because there is a lot of shame and pain surrounding them. Those who have never felt depression often cannot understand what it feels like or how it happens. I have rarely talked about my experience with depression, but this chapter is about messengers and the miracles that can come from them. I closed this chapter of my life a long time ago, but I am ready to share my story and acknowledge that sometimes life is incredibly hard. The year these events unfolded turned out to be the most important year of my life. I received an amazing gift one summer from a stranger who was my messenger. If you are depressed and feel like nothing will ever change, I hope my story will show you that there is always hope— for everyone and every situation.

Up until the age of forty I had depressive episodes. They started as a teenager and came and went randomly. As time went on, I realized it was emotional stressors that triggered them. If it was just one thing in my life veering off course, I was fine, but if multiple things were going wrong, negative feelings and vitriolic self-talk would emerge and I would descend into a funk. That was what I came to call these episodes. I had a lot of negative thoughts that would play in my mind on an endless loop. The message said, "Marilyn, you are a failure and there is no need to continue your life. All you do is make mistakes, and I don't see that ever changing."

This was the never-ending message I would hear during an episode, and it was my biggest burden and darkest secret. As is the case with many families, we were never encouraged to talk about our feelings. Fast forward to adulthood and there was no way I could share my problem; it felt too risky to divulge something so painful and private. I might sound "crazy" if I shared it. (the tape playing in your mind says to do what?) It felt safer to keep quiet and struggle alone. What was the struggle during an episode? Try to imagine the worst day of your life: absolutely nothing goes right, and you are overwhelmed with unrelenting negative thoughts about yourself. I felt like I was drowning in feelings of hopelessness. From my journal dated August 5, 2000, "When I'm low, I'm so low, it's scary—no energy, no love of life. Everything is bleak."

These funks would usually last two or three days, then lift for a week, a month, or even a year. When I was in a funk, I couldn't think of one redeeming quality I possessed—not one. I look back now and think, "How could I have been in such a dark place?" Depression has been described as tunnel vision. I was once again trapped in that dark place when I wrote this poem. I was thirty-eight years old.

March 31, 2000

Flowers, wind and colors—these things make my life feel real. Books to make my mind calm down; give me a reason to live, to go on, and not give up—to want to be here one more day. These are the things that make me want to stay.

A kind smile, which I return, a helping hand that calms my nerves. I bless you as I walk away. These are things that make me stay. I want to be whole, to heal myself. I'll never do it if I run away. When my sadness pulls me down, I quietly plead, "Let me go—I want to go. I'm so tired of feeling this way." But my soul hangs on, looks down the road and sees I have a ways to go. "You've tried so hard, don't give up" it seems to whisper, as I stubbornly asked to be erased. "Take me off this page—I give you permission!" But I'm still here. Even though I am tired, I go on.

I was grappling with these episodes and trying to keep it together, but I also knew it was too big for me to solve by myself. Knowing that this problem was not going to go away, I went to Kaiser and discussed it with my doctor. He suggested Prozac and counseling and I agreed to both. After three months of visiting the therapist they had assigned me, I asked, "Why don't I feel any better?" She replied, "You're on the lowest dose of Prozac. You won't feel better till we raise the dosage." I was stunned. Why hadn't she told me that, and why hadn't they raised the dosage by now? I felt like she was just going through the motions in our therapy sessions. We didn't have a rapport and without that, counseling doesn't work. Feeling sorely disappointed and having lost faith in Kaiser, I stopped all treatment. I was engulfed in something not allowing me to think clearly and I only saw things in terms of black and white. Welcome to the world of depression.

I hate to admit this, but I don't specifically remember praying for help. I do remember times walking down the street and thinking how I could end it. I only lived ten minutes from the Golden Gate Bridge, and I knew it was possible to jump off the bridge in certain spots. At least that's what I'd heard. I found out many years later this is called suicidal ideation. Looking back, I realize that asking for my life to end was my prayer for help.

I have always felt a special connection with my grandma Clara—my mom's mother. As a child, she would visit us every other month and occasionally spend the night at our house. She felt at home in the kitchen and soon after arriving, she would find an apron and start baking; coffee cake, loaves of bread, or a pie. I would grab a chair to stand on so I could watch her and help out. She loved to tell stories of when she lived on our farm. She talked about the days of horse and buggies, and Grandpa Joe and their neighbors making moonshine during prohibition. She enjoyed walking around the property, and she would ask me to go with her. The farm that I grew up on was the farm she and Grandpa had bought as newlyweds back in 1920. They had planted many of the big trees that were in our yard and cleared the fields that are used to this day for crops. The one-on-one time she spent with me was cherished—she always made me feel special. She passed away when I was twenty-two years old. When I was going through these periods of depression, I would find myself dreaming of her and thinking of her often. I came to realize her spirit was close by. I remember writing in my journal, "I'm thinking about her all the time; I know she's around me." I believe she was trying to help me remember that I was loved—and to not give up.

Hello Messenger

In the summer, I would often leave the cold fog in San Francisco and visit warmer places. While on a weekend getaway, I discovered a place I grew to love. I began driving up to Harbin Hot Springs to relax. It's a beautiful spot north of Calistoga, California. It is remote and quiet with natural mineral springs of varying temperatures. Long ago, it was a sacred, spiritual place inhabited by the Native Americans in that area. Then as now, it's a place where people come to reflect and meditate. It has always had a spiritual vibe and attracted people who were interested in meditating, healing, and holistic lifestyles.

An interesting thing happened one summer evening. I was hanging out in one of the warm pools and I struck up a conversation with a man named John who lived in the Bay area. He told me about a friend of his who was a social worker and who had learned a therapeutic technique he and other clinicians called light therapy. This form of therapy purportedly had cured people with depression and many other mental disorders, including PTSD. He was treating people in a safe but unconventional way. This was not the same light therapy treatment used to treat SAD, or seasonal affective disorder. John had tried it and he highly recommended it. He explained the technique and told me the sessions were $60.00. I asked him, "How many would I need?" He told me his friend Deiter recommended six to eight sessions. I was very interested in trying it, so I took his contact information. I did not have the extra money at the time, so I put the idea on the back burner. I remember feeling hopeful and excited that perhaps I had found something that would help me.

The Visitor

Less than two weeks later, my older sister Pat from Indiana called me out of the blue. She told me she had promised a friend of hers, Linda, that she could stay with me in San Francisco. Linda needed to visit San Francisco every six months to check on her elderly mother. My sister did not ask if I wanted to host her friend. She was very matter of fact and explained the situation, giving me the dates of her friend's trip. I had mixed feelings about Linda coming to stay with me because I had never met her. In fact, Pat had never even mentioned her to me until this conversation. The truth was, I was very annoyed that my sister had insisted upon it, instead of asking me as a favor. After discussing it, I told her it would be fine. The following day I did what my mom always taught us to do when company is coming: I cleaned my apartment.

Linda knocked on my door a few days later. When I opened the door, I instantly liked her. She was a kind, sweet person who anyone would want to help. She was easy to talk to and we became fast friends. We went out to dinner one night and another night she came with me to sing karaoke at my favorite spot. She was too shy to get up and sing, but I introduced her to my karaoke friends, and she fit right in. I was really happy my sister had suggested she stay with me. When it came time for her to leave, I told her she had to stay with me on her next visit. We hugged goodbye and she left for the airport.

Shortly afterwards, I noticed an envelope on the kitchen table. When I opened it, there was $300.00 in cash. I was stunned. My first thought was, "Why did she do this? She was staying with me to save money!" My second thought was, "Now I can do the light therapy!" What an incredibly generous thing she did. The Law of Attraction was at work. I was thinking about the light therapy and I believed it was worth trying, but I didn't know how I was going to get the money. There is a mantra I learned many years ago, **"Everything is working in my favor now."** I say this mantra when I want to bring something new into my life *and* when I see positive things happening. All things *were* working in my favor now, and I was not going to ignore this opportunity. For things to change in our lives, we need to be open to guidance, and given the chance, we **must** act on those opportunities.

The Treatment

I immediately made an appointment for a light therapy session. Deiter was a licensed social worker and was very interested in holistic medicine and alternative treatments. He had been trained to use the light therapy machine from another therapist in the Bay area. Dieter had treated many people and based on their feedback, he believed 100% in its ability to help and heal them.

Over the next three months, I had seven sessions with him. The sessions were about twenty to thirty minutes long. The session began by him explaining how the equipment worked and why I would be hooked up to a computer. He showed me the glasses, which were a special pair of wraparound oversized sunglasses. The treatments involved wearing the glasses during the session. Attached to the inside of the glasses were wires and small lights. When the machine was turned on, the lights blinked, penetrating your eyes. They were not bright and did not cause any discomfort.

Then he attached electrode wires to my forehead. All of this was hooked up to a computer, which was recording my brain waves. The actual light sessions were brief. The first one was only five minutes in length, and each subsequent session became longer. He said that most people had no reaction to the treatment while it was happening. However, they would report that as time went on, their symptoms would dissipate. I wanted desperately to be free of those depressive episodes, but I wondered, "Will I feel any different after I finish the therapy? Could this treatment really work?"

A few months after the treatments ended, I remember walking down a street in San Francisco and feeling…..different. I felt lighter and happier. I asked myself, "Is it my imagination or do I really feel better?" It's hard to put into words, but my body felt ethereal and my mind was at peace. I had forgotten what it felt like to feel this good. I couldn't stop smiling because I felt so happy. That afternoon stands out as the defining moment when I realized the light therapy had worked. Could I prove it objectively? No—but I had a strong intuitive hunch, and I was learning to trust those gut feelings more and more.

I honestly never thought those funks would completely stop. For several years, I held my breath and waited for something in my life to trigger an episode. In the years since the treatment, I've had many stressful events in my life, but I've never had another depressive episode. I never experienced another funk and the negative tapes never played again. This is how I know it worked. Even now, I'm amazed that the light therapy eradicated my depression.

John was my messenger and our encounter changed my life. If you believe in serendipity, it was not chance. Why did John and I start talking about light therapy that night in the pool? There were countless things we could have talked about that evening, yet he was prompted to tell me his story about light therapy. I trust and believe it was Spirit reaching out to help me. Three pivotal people came into my life that year: John, Linda, and Dieter. It's as though their energy triangulated in a miraculous way to heal me; to restore the peace I'd lost. This is one of the things I love about life. We never know what is coming down the road. Sometimes, it's something wonderful!

A Different Message

Several years after the light therapy sessions, I flew back to Michigan to attend my mom's funeral. Her funeral was difficult as my whole family struggled to accept our monumental loss. It was the day I'd been dreading my entire life; saying goodbye to my mom. As I was sitting in the church waiting for the funeral to begin, I heard a voice say, "This is the way it was supposed to be—you were supposed to be at her funeral, not the other way around." I knew it was true. I thank God I was given a second chance at life—one without depression. Light therapy gave me the lasting peace I never thought I would have. I will be forever grateful to Spirit for sending me a messenger on that beautiful summer night all those years ago.

And my grandma Clara? Since those dark days, I rarely feel her presence around me, although she pops into my head and my dreams occasionally. She visited me a few years ago in a dream. She was a young woman about twenty years old, and by looking into her eyes, I recognized her. She stood there smiling at me but never spoke a word. She had such an adoring look of love on her face, I wanted to reach out and touch her, but I was afraid I would break the spell and end the dream. Feeling courageous, I put my hand out to hers and she reached back and touched mine. It was nothing less than amazing, because in her presence I felt completely engulfed in love. In the end, love is all there is.

Your Messenger

We all go through periods in our life where we feel lost and alone. I believe that when you pray or ask for help— from God, from angels, or even from your relatives who have passed, you will be given it in one form or another. We are not always aware of it, but it's interesting how often we will find a book, an article, or a messenger who will present us with information that will guide us where we need to go. Having faith and being open to receive is very important when we are working through these difficult situations. When we're receptive, Spirit will find a way to give us our answers. Messages can come to us in countless ways; conversations, dreams, spontaneous thoughts, a pod cast, a TED talk, and more. Be open-minded regarding the messenger because you never know how or when it may happen. I am proof that no matter how low we sink, we can come back from it and live a life with peace and happiness.

Dieter and John called the therapy I had "light therapy" because it used lights, but I don't believe that was its real name. Since Deiter passed away in 2011, I couldn't ask him for background information on it. In doing research for the book, I looked for information on a therapy that mirrored the kind I had participated in. I was treated with only one color of light, but I was healed from the light therapy. When reading about Emotional Transformational Therapy, it seems to be very similar to the type of therapy I received from Dieter.

Emotional Transformational Therapy

ETT is a therapeutic method incorporating the use of light, color wavelengths, and eye movements, and it aims to rapidly transform emotional distress and related physical pain into a positive emotional state. (Goodtherapy.org) Dr. Steven Vazquez is credited with creating Emotional Transformational Therapy in 1991. His non-invasive and non-pharmaceutical approach combines traditional psychotherapy with the use of visual brain stimulation and colored light therapy. This works to reshape the neural impulses affecting the brain and the nervous system. (Goodtherapy.org) He is the author of a book based on his research, *Emotional Transformation Therapy & Accelerated Ecological Therapy.* ETT may be used to treat the following: depression, post-traumatic stress, anxiety, phobias, panic, chronic physical pain, and attention deficit hypcractivity. Therapists using this modality of treatment say their patients make a dramatic recovery in a short amount of time—sometimes eight to ten sessions. Many patients also report they stop needing prescription drugs after participating in the therapy.

Dr. Vazquez works in Austin, Texas and trains therapists in Emotional Transformational Therapy all over the United States. You can look up goodtherapy.org and search for therapists in your area trained in ETT. There are many other resources online where you can learn more about Emotional Transformation Therapy.

EMDR Therapy

EMDR or Eye Movement Desensitization and Reprocessing is a form of psychotherapy that enables people to heal from the symptoms and emotional distress that result from traumatic life experiences. EMDR therapy shows that the mind can be healed from psychological trauma much in the same way our body recovers from physical trauma. EMDR therapy focuses directly on the memory and is intended to change the way that the memory is stored in the brain, thus reducing and eliminating the problematic symptoms. (apa.org)

What exactly is EMDR? According to emdr-training.net, EMDR therapy is founded on the basis that our emotional well-being is interwoven with our physical (somatic) state. EMDR employs a body-based technique called bilateral simulation during which a therapist will guide a client through eye movements, tones, or taps in order to move a memory that has been incorrectly stored to a more functional part of the brain. During trauma, our brain processes and stores memories incorrectly. This therapy corrects the mis-storage so that the painful memories associated with the trauma lose their charge.

"More than 30 positive controlled outcome studies have been done on EMDR therapy. Some of the studies show that 84%-90% of single trauma victims no longer have post-traumatic stress disorder after only three 90-minute sessions. A study done by HMO Kaiser Permanente found that 77% of multiple trauma victims no longer were diagnosed with PTSD after only six fifty minute sessions. In another study, 77% of combat veterans were free of PTSD in 12 sessions. There has been so much research on EMDR therapy that now it is recognized as an effective form of treatment for trauma and other disturbing experiences by organizations such as the American Psychiatric Association, the World Health Organization, and the Department of Defense. Millions of people have been treated successfully over the past 25 years." (emdr.com) According to the American Psychiatric Association, EMDR may be particularly useful to people who have trouble talking about the traumatic events they've experienced.

EMDR has been proven to help people suffering from many mental disorders, including: PTSD (post-traumatic stress disorder), panic attacks, phobias, addictions, sexual or physical abuse, personality disorders, dissociative disorders, and more. Many people report their symptoms are greatly reduced or completely eliminated in six to twelve sessions. The number of sessions for each individual will depend on the level of trauma being treated. On emdria.org there is additional information and resources to find a therapist in your area. I am a big believer in the philosophy of "keep on trying" until you find a something that works for you.

Another resource is the confidential **National Suicide Prevention Lifeline**. You call toll free: **1-800-273-TALK.** (8255) 24 hours a day/7 days a week.

We trust that Spirit guides us and miracles happen.

Chapter 4: The Power of Thoughts and Words

The Power of Positive Self Talk

Before the light therapy, I was my own worst critic. If something didn't work out, I believed it was most likely my fault. In the months that followed the light therapy, I began to notice something: I was thinking and acting differently. I wasn't so quick to assign blame to myself for everything, and when I did make a mistake, I wasn't nearly as upset about it. In addition to feeling lighter and happier, I got to ride a second wave of positivity when I realized I was acting a lot nicer to everyone, especially myself. I was still having one-sided conversations, but this time it was different. I found myself saying positive things like, "You're doing great, girl!" and "You look really cute today!" I even remember hanging out in my apartment in San Francisco on Saturday mornings and saying to myself, "I love you." That might sound weird for me to say and even admit, but I had never felt that way, let alone said it to myself—EVER. Somehow I knew it was a milestone for me—like I had graduated from a dysfunctional group into an emotionally healthy one. These thoughts started happening almost spontaneously. I don't believe I made a conscious decision to start doing this in the beginning. When I would do something dumb like lock myself out of my apartment, instead of getting angry with myself, I would stay calm and try to figure out a solution. It didn't mushroom into a "how could you be so stupid?" scenario like it had in the past.

One time, I switched purses because I was going on a date and wanted to carry a small vintage handbag. I sat in my hallway and sorted through my larger purse to grab the few things I really needed. As I was leaving, to save time I stepped outside and locked the door from the inside, then shut it. Then it hit me: "Where are my keys?" I knew instantly—they were on a shelf in my hallway where I had laid them. My apartment was located on the second floor. There was a large kitchen window that was about four feet off the ground facing a small landing. I had plants sitting on a low bench just under the window. I reached up and pushed on it to see if by chance I had left the window unlocked. It began to slide up and I immediately thanked God for this lucky break! I was able to hoist myself up onto the windowsill and crawl up inside the kitchen window. Problem solved, "Good job, Marilyn!"

I began to witness a transformation in myself. Have you noticed the amount of patience we have for ourselves is equal to the amount we have for others? Before light therapy, I did not have a lot of patience with myself, especially if I made a mistake. The tendency to quickly find fault and blame myself for something was deeply ingrained in me. It was second nature to wield that faultfinding knife at others too. Now that habit was quickly fading into my past, and instead, I was creating an upward spiral; a phenomenon I had never experienced before. The more loving kindness I saw in myself, the more I liked Marilyn, and all of this made me more aware of the person I wanted to be, not just intermittently, but 24/7: calm, kind, and loving. It bolstered me to continue on with my personal affirmations and it just kept building. I intuitively knew those affirmations were helping me feel lighter and happier. I don't have to tell you—life felt easier.

When we are thinking good thoughts about ourselves, it shows in our self-confidence. We look happier because we are. I love a quote by Audrey Hepburn, "Happiest girls are the prettiest." We can expand that thought by saying, "Happiest people are the prettiest." Love, whether it's self-love or love directed towards others, makes everyone look and feel beautiful.

Accepting and loving myself has made a huge difference in my life. After fifteen years of practicing positive self-talk, it's second nature now. I use self-talk throughout the day, every day. I'm supportive of myself when things are going great, and I'm forgiving when they are not. Now, when I finish a job like cleaning the house or yard work, I'll say to myself, "Good job, girl!" When I make a mistake, I'll tell myself, "Don't worry, it's all going to be fine." This happened recently when I was driving in an unfamiliar area of Orange County, California and I missed my exit. I was annoyed that I had missed it because it's a very busy freeway and it meant I had to go up to the next exit and double back. In spite of this, I did not get mad or upset. Instead, I said, "It's not a big deal." There is something about hearing everything is going to be okay that's comforting, even if I'm the one saying it. It only takes a second and it doesn't cost a thing. We all develop coping skills in life and this one is great because its positive effects are felt immediately.

If you don't do it yet, I hope you'll try it sometime. If you mess something up, you can say to yourself, "It's okay, everyone makes mistakes and shit happens." Any positive statement to remind yourself that you love and forgive yourself is all that's needed. Please don't beat yourself up when you make a mistake. It's much easier to fix the error if possible, apologize, and move on. Always forgive yourself because no one is perfect. No one is perfect. These are the kind of habits and coping skills we want to cultivate; ones that show love and forgiveness to others and ourselves, are easy to implement, and give positive results.

Mistakes

I've learned some important lessons since my light therapy. As much as I enjoy being a cheerleader for others, I need to be one for myself too!!! Positive self-talk is like having our own cheerleader. I once lost my favorite scarf made of black Mongolian lamb. It was beautiful, soft, and looked great with whatever I was wearing. I was very annoyed because I couldn't remember where I'd lost it, and it became that nagging, unresolved issue on my mind. I racked my brain trying to remember where I might have left it, since I have a bad habit of leaving something behind more often than not. I asked everyone I knew if they had seen it and to keep an eye out for it, but it never turned up. Its disappearance was a mystery.

Eventually I went to Plan B: replacing it. I wanted it to be identical to the one I'd lost, so I looked everywhere trying to find the same color and length, but it was not available. I even went back to the original store, Loehmann's, but they no longer carried it. In the old days I would have called myself an idiot and really vilified myself for losing something so special. It would have bothered me for weeks, but I was changing and decided to be nice to myself. Instead, I said, "Don't worry, I'll replace it for you no matter how long it takes." That act of kindness towards myself made me feel so much better. The truth is, we all make mistakes. We don't need to be so hard on ourselves. Isn't that how we learn in life? In the end, I let it go and knew that finding another one would remain unfinished business until another time or I decided it was no longer important.

The Reverb Effect

As I've become practiced in patience and forgiveness, it's become easy to offer my students the same grace and forgiveness I give myself. At school, kids sometimes spill their milk when they're eating. It creates a big mess and yes, it's a bit of a pain to clean up. I used to get slightly annoyed with having to deal with it. I made a conscious decision that I was not going to react that way anymore. I began to tell the kids, "Close your milk carton at the top so you don't make a milk lake." They would all smile and many would laugh at the absurdity, saying, "There's no such thing as a milk lake!" When someone would spill it, another child would invariably say, "Look! A milk lake!" We'd all laugh together, and I'd say, "What? How did that happen?" It's all very lighthearted and they know I am not upset about it. Making a good-natured joke about a mistake is a great way to diffuse the situation.

Changing the Pattern

In order to stop negative self-talk, we must first become aware of it. Start noticing what you say to yourself when something goes wrong. If you are criticizing, berating, or complaining, you are making the situation worse. Instead, stop and think of another way to look at the situation. When I am stuck in traffic because I left work twenty minutes late, instead of bemoaning the situation, I'll tell myself, "I guess I'm meant to slow down and see other things." I'll start to notice the landscape, the neighborhood, or the person walking their dog. It's a shift in perspective I'm choosing because I don't want to feel agitated or annoyed.

When things aren't going well in our lives, it's easy to get stuck in the negative self-talk rut. We see a (perceived) negative quality or situation and tell ourselves we're unlovable or we become hypercritical of ourselves. I was a master at this when I was in a funk. Maybe we've gained some weight, or someone has broken up with us. Our boss may have recently given us a bad review, or we're having a rough year all around. Here are a few things people say when they're feeling bad about themselves.

1. I'm so fat/ugly/stupid—no one will ever love me.

2. I'm a loser—no one would want to date or marry me.

3. My career sucks—I'll never be successful.

4. I'm unlucky in love.

5. I'll be alone for the rest of my life.

6. I'll never have what I want in life.

7. I don't deserve happiness.

8. I am unlovable.

These are false beliefs we tell ourselves: lies. If the Law of Attraction says we bring into our lives what we think about, how will we ever get what we want (love) with negative thoughts? It will be impossible. When your mind starts to go down the rabbit hole of negative thinking, you must stop it in its tracks and supplant it with something else—something positive. *You must interrupt the pattern of negative thinking.*

The Merriam-Webster dictionary defines a mantra as: a sound, word, or phrase that is repeated by someone who is praying or meditating. Mantras are nothing more than us aligning and guiding our thoughts where we want them to go. To get results, it is recommended to say mantras anytime, anywhere, day or night. More positive thoughts = more positive results. You could replace any of those negative thoughts with something positive in the form of a mantra:

1. I am beautiful and lovable just the way I am.

2. I deserve to be happy and loved.

3. I attract great people with great energy into my life.

4. I give love, respect, and kindness to people and it is returned in kind.

5. I can create anything I want in life.

6. All my dreams are coming true now.

You can also create your own mantra. Just make sure you state things in the affirmative, not the negative. We don't create mantras like, "I don't want to be alone in life." Instead we could say, "I share my life with people I love and who love me." State mantras in the positive because that's what works. *Change always starts with our attitude and our thoughts.* Choose consciously to think nice things about yourself and believe in your ability to create anything you want. Mantras help us channel our focus on what we want to create.

One of my favorite self-created mantras is, "It's a beautiful day to be alive." When I'm standing out on the tennis courts or taking a walk and it's a lovely day, it strikes me as the perfect thought for that moment. It's an expression of gratitude and it makes me happy! That is what life is all about: being happy.

Mantras Make a Difference

Émile Coué was a French pharmacologist who worked with patients in France around the turn of the twentieth century. He was trained to dispense prescription medication and he noticed that when he would tell his patients how well a drug worked, they would often come back later telling him of the great results and healing they had experienced. He would also give them a mantra to say. When he would say nothing about a drugs' efficacy and offered no mantra, he noticed those patients came back with a lot more complaints about their health. Did the patients given a mantra heal themselves with positive thoughts?

When we *believe* something will make us better, often our belief is the catalyst that improves our condition. Doctors call this the placebo effect. This phenomenon has been proven many times in double blind studies. A double blind study is often used by drug companies and in psychological experiments so researchers can control the environment. Let's say there are two groups of people participating in a cancer drug trial. One group will be given the actual drug, and the second group will be given a placebo. Neither the subjects participating, nor the researchers know who is getting the drug and who is getting the placebo. There are many studies showing people in the placebo group reporting they feel better, their symptoms have subsided, and other positive effects. They often show the same improvement as those who actually took the test drug. Did their body heal on its own or did their thoughts contribute to their healing? Prayers, mantras, and positive thoughts; they all work together to heal us.

Mantras and Goals

Mr. Coué gave his patients several mantras, but this one was the most used, **"Every day in every way, I am getting better and better."** This is a powerful mantra to use if you've had health issues and are working towards getting back to 100%, but it's also great to keep a positive vibe flowing throughout the day. He asked his patients to say it twenty times a day, in the morning and evening. He believed the bewitching hour when we are waking up and drifting off to sleep was when people were most likely to influence their subconscious mind. I say it whenever I think about it!

Mantras can have a profound effect on changing our lives because thoughts really are mind over matter. We're stating in the affirmative what we want to create and bring into our lives. One mantra I've used for many years is, "Thank you for my healthy body and strong mind." Or, I'll say, "Thank you for my strong body and healthy mind." I'm in good health and I want to keep reinforcing it with positive thoughts. But saying a mantra alone is not always enough to change something—we must also **take action**. To stay healthy, I take action by exercising and watching what I eat. I know fresh fruits and vegetables are the healthiest, so I try to eat them every day. Processed foods and foods full of sugar taste good and are convenient, but they're not helping any of us stay healthy. I eat desserts once in awhile, but not every day or even every week. These small daily choices regarding diet and exercise will cumulatively add up to good or poor health down the road. Think about what kind of lifestyle you want ten or twenty years from now. Do you want to feel good and be able to walk, bike, and move without pain every day? None of us want to be on costly medications that have side effects also affecting our quality of life. Our choices today will determine if we are healthy in twenty or thirty years. My mom lived with Type 2 diabetes for over forty years, and it took a huge toll on her health and eventually, her quality of life. My goal is to stay healthy so I will never have to deal with diabetes. My other goal is to be playing tennis in my eighties! I want to be able to move and feel good, regardless of my age.

Whether we are in perfect health or not, we can say positive things to help us set goals and then make choices that will help us meet those goals. **The positive statements + the positive actions = results. (The Law**

of Attraction) Because I find it peaceful and healthy, I go for a walk every day if possible. My goal is thirty to forty minutes, but if I can only get in fifteen to twenty minutes, I'll say to myself, "That's great! You did a twenty-minute walk!" These affirmations are both rewarding and reinforcing me to keep up the good work.

Our thoughts affect us far more than we realize. Once we become aware of any negative thinking, we can change it to something positive. Awareness is key. Remember: You are powerful, you are a creator, and you are a healer. Hold on to all your good thoughts because that energy is touching everyone and it's creating a wonderful reverb effect among the rest of us.

When we choose positive thoughts,

we are healing the world.

Chapter 5: Children, Be My Teacher

Children are a gift to us. Do you know why? In their faces you will see pure love and joy. Their presence reminds us that love exists, love is magical, and it's within us waiting to be expressed. We can learn or relearn many of life's lessons from a child.

* Children are trusting.

* Children are forgiving.

* Children are love.

* Children live in the moment.

* Children are in awe of nature, beauty, and joy.

* Children don't hold a grudge.

* Children are excited by new experiences.

* Children appreciate any kind gesture and will often reciprocate in some way.

Working with children has given me so much joy. I give them unconditional love and it is returned to me every day. Children of all ages show courage, vulnerability, fortitude, and joy every day. How many of us do that on a regular basis? Our mission as adults is to guide them and nurture these qualities they naturally possess. They help us remember what's important and I feel honored to be in their presence. Children represent the future and planting seeds of love begins with us caring for them.

Unconditional Love

You will never spoil someone by loving him or her too much. Loving them does not mean showering them with gifts on their birthdays or bribing them with toys or visits to Chuck E. Cheese when you want them to listen to you or because you feel guilty because you work full time. I'm talking about accepting and loving them for who they are. Each child is totally unique, and with your love and acceptance they will discover what gifts they've brought into the world to share.

Encourage them to pursue whatever interests they have, even if it seems silly or unimportant to you. Spirit will be guiding them as they grow and find their way. When we accept them for who they are and love them unconditionally, we are helping them become happy and confident adults. Let's model for them the qualities of acceptance, tolerance, and kindness, so they will learn to treat others with the same consideration. What will our world look like when we have millions of young adults who embody those qualities? It will be a world where you'll see people helping people regardless of race or culture, people working together to solve problems, and a generation *whose actions* will demonstrate they care about our planet and every living thing here.

Molding Us for Better or for Worse

Wouldn't it be amazing if we could remember the day we were born? Some people say they remember events from their childhood that happened when they were two or three years old. Many more of us have clear memories starting around the age of four. It's been said that everything that happens to us is recorded in our subconscious mind. I picture it as two proverbial buckets sitting in there. Every time someone is kind, loving, or caring, a drop of love goes into the bucket. Every time someone hurts us or causes pain, a drop of pain goes into that bucket. As we go through our childhood, the process continues 24/7 without fail, with *everything* being recorded. Later as adults, it is still happening, but it is having a lesser effect on us. Let's say all of those events of love and pain are recorded and stored deep in our subconscious. Now what? The children and adults who have an *abundance of love* recorded will be the happiest and most well-adjusted. Overall, they will feel content with who they are, and they'll feel secure as adults. They will not feel the need to hurt others. When they do experience a setback or someone hurts them, they can handle it and move on, because they have a positive opinion of themselves. They have coping skills because they have an unshakable belief that they are loved and valued. Their intrinsic core beliefs about themselves and the world are positive ones.

People who have survived traumas; (physical, emotional, and sexual abuse) will have many more drops of pain in their bucket and it will be evident. As children, they often have very low self-esteem, do poorly in school, and disrespect others as they act out their emotions destructively. They may turn their anger and sadness inward and try to hurt themselves, or they may express it outwardly by trying to hurt others verbally and physically. Those who have been sexually abused often will act out the abuse and victimize someone else.

Twenty years ago, I worked in program that served emotionally disturbed children who because of their emotional dis-regulation, could only handle being in their classroom for a half day. They attended our program from 12:00 p.m. to 3:00 p.m. daily. The ratio was 8:2 student/teachers. Most of their home situations were extremely dysfunctional and all of them were still living with one or both parents. One five-year-old boy was always on the verge of exploding in anger and his twelve-year-old brother had already attempted suicide. Another girl was ten and her mom was always threatening to take her and her brother to the orphanage to live because they were "bad." She shared other details with me as well. Her five-year-old brother had more issues than her. He had suffered some kind of accident and had a very large jagged scar across his scalp. I never knew how that had happened, but it looked like a major trauma. Another girl in third grade would start screaming at the top of her lungs for no apparent reason and would throw whatever objects were around. I heard rumors her mom had been in a satanic cult, but this was never substantiated. At their young ages, my students were already showing signs of severe mental duress. I spoke to my supervisors about contacting Child Protective Services, but they said we had no information to report that would warrant CPS removing the children from their homes. Children don't get removed just because they have lousy parents. There are always exceptions and some people do overcome their dysfunctional childhoods to create a happy life for themselves, but sadly, many more do not.

Lost Souls

Prisons are filled with people who were abused in countless ways, many from an early age. The majority of them also grew up in poverty. Their needs of being protected, loved, and cherished were not met in childhood and they have paid the price. As a society we have also paid the price. This is why I advocate for programs that give lower income children support like free preschool, free tutoring, free lunches, counseling, and other programs that help support the child within the family unit. We can pay on the front end to get children on track or we can pay on the back end, when they end up as high school dropouts, unemployed, or incarcerated.

It's much more cost effective and rewarding for everyone to pay on the front end and help those children in need. I've worked with families earning over $100,000 per year and families living in poverty on a small disability check. We know the playing field is not level for every child growing up. The child from the poor family is just as charming, smart, and deserving as the child from the other family, yet the deck is stacked against him or her disproportionately. For families who cannot afford to pay for preschool, subsidized programs like Head Start and State preschools offer wonderful opportunities in early childhood education. The programs meet the children's needs in so many ways; social emotional support, modeling language and listening skills, fine and gross motor development, and pre-academic skills in literacy, math, and science. All of this is preparing them for success in kindergarten and beyond. They begin kindergarten with a positive attitude and a solid foundation in school readiness.

Last summer, I was at a flea market in Michigan and decided to eat lunch there. I sat down at some picnic tables next to a young woman named Tia and her grandma and we began chatting. After lunch, the grandma wandered off and she and I continued talking. As the conversation meandered, she shared with me that she worked as a stripper. I had never met a stripper before, so I began asking her questions. Maybe it was the combination of being a good listener and showing genuine interest that made her comfortable in sharing her story.

Tia told me about her regular customers (all the girls have them) and the thousands of dollars in cash she and the other dancers earned every week. She told me about the rampant drug and alcohol abuse among strippers. She said, "Most girls get high because it's easier to strip when you are." I asked her what her grandma thought about her stripping and if she knew about it. "Yeah, she knows. She don't like it, but I help pay her rent and I give her money too." She added, "I don't really enjoy it, but it's easy money."

After awhile, she confided she had a problem with drug addiction, and she was planning to go into rehab later that month. She had a sister in North Carolina whom she was close to who was helping to arrange it. It was none of my business, but I asked why she had started taking drugs. Her answer was disconcerting, "I had a bad childhood. My dad used to tell us he was going to put rat poison in our food and kill us." In that moment it's hard to know how to respond to a young woman who is explaining why her life is already off the rails at age twenty-five. One can only imagine what other traumatic events she endured as a child. Rest assured, those drugs were helping her cope with the fallout of her dysfunctional family and the bad memories still haunting her.

Some people would have looked down on her for her lifestyle and her choices. I saw a young woman struggling to find her way in the world and masking a lot of pain with drug use. By agreeing to rehab, she was trying to get better, and I give her a lot of credit for that. I pray she was successful in beating her drug addiction and finding peace.

Planting Positive Seeds

I do everything possible to be positive and loving with my students. I want to add lots of love to their buckets. They won't remember all the details of their time spent in my class, but they will have happy memories of preschool. When I ask parents what their children say about school, the answer I most often hear is, "They love school and they can't wait to come every day." Some parents tell me their children cry on weekends because they want to come to school. This feedback shows me they are happy to come to school and learn. I want them to have a positive experience they will carry with them into kindergarten and beyond. I am creating the blueprint for their future education and I take it seriously. I have fond memories of my years in elementary school because I had many teachers who cared. I also had wonderful neighbors, Girl Scout leaders, and relatives who were supportive and kind.

I know they helped shape me into someone who could trust others and see the glass as half full in life.

The generation of children growing up now will have the opportunity to shift the energy of our planet away from negativity, fear, and disconnection because they are bringing in the vibration of peace, love, and knowingness that "we're all one." Can you see how in twenty years things could look so differently? *Children are the answer* and we need to give them all the love and support they deserve.

There is a verse from the book of Mark in the Bible, which I really love.

Mark 10:14 – But when Jesus saw it he was indignant and said to them, "See that you do not despise one of these little ones. For I tell you that in heaven, their angels always see the face of my father who is in heaven."

Large Gifts Come in Small Packages

Last year, I had a boy in my class named Ramell. He was four and a half when he joined my class. He had deep soulful eyes, a beautiful smile, and an amazing capacity for tenderness. Ramell was wonderful to all the children in class—helpful and kind. I never saw him get angry. On the first day of school, another boy named Adrian began crying as his dad was saying goodbye. Ramell saw him crying and immediately went up to him and put his arm around him to comfort him. I was surprised because he had never met the boy before. These two boys became very good friends and were close throughout the school year.

Midway through the year, a boy transferred to my class named Justin. He was socially awkward and did not make much eye contact nor did he initiate any conversations. On top of that, he had many allergies and his nose was constantly running. His allergies made him sneeze a lot. Although he was five, he didn't know how to blow his nose, so we were always helping him. The other kids felt like he was different, and he was. When the other teacher or I would ask him something, he either wouldn't answer, or he would mumble something. Because of all this, the other children did not interact with him much; in fact, they mostly ignored him. I worried that Justin had developmental delays because he seemed so disconnected from his environment.

I spoke to his parents about my concerns. His parents loved him but based on what they shared, I surmised he was not getting the quality time and attention from them he desperately needed. They allowed him to watch YouTube videos and movies for hours and when we asked Justin what he was watching, he talked about a lot of adult content (violent movies) not suitable for children. His mom told me the reason they had put him in school was because he was not talking at home. She said, "I thought something was wrong with him." I almost put in a referral for him to be assessed, but I decided to wait and give him some time.

A month went by and I did not see a lot of improvement. I knew I needed to do an intervention, so I decided to try something different. I asked Ramell and two other boys to join me in the quiet area of our classroom. I chose them because not only were they emotionally mature, they were smart and articulate as well. They were the perfect role models for Justin. Even though they were young, I felt they might grasp the concept of helping someone through friendship. They all sat on a small blue couch and I sat down across from them. The first thing I asked was, "Do you like playing with Justin?"

Ramell answered, "No."

Adrian hesitantly replied, "Yes," and Juan didn't answer.

I told them that Justin was going to kindergarten like them, but he wasn't quite ready. They looked at me, and then Adrian asked, "Am I ready?"

"Yes," I replied. Then the other two boys asked the same question and I reassured them, "Yes, all of you are ready." So often, children need our reassurance more than we realize.

Looking at them intently I said, "I think all of you can help Justin. Will you play with him occasionally during free choice so he can practice sharing and using his words?" I waited for a response. They all had that look on their faces. It's the look people give you when they don't know how to respond. I knew they wanted to please me, but they were also feeling ambivalent, because they did not see him as someone they would enjoy playing with. Although none of them expressed much enthusiasm over the suggestion, they agreed they would try. I wasn't convinced this would work or that they would even remember our conversation the following week. If they didn't reach out to him, I wasn't going to bring it up again.

About a week later, I noticed Ramell and Adrian playing with Justin outside by the monkey bars. Justin didn't know how to cross the monkey bars, so he was standing on the edge of the platform, closely watching them. When the two boys would pass by, they'd tickle him gently, similar to how we tickle babies. Justin responded by laughing and smiling in a way I had never seen before. He had a look of pure joy on his chubby face. Soon he began tickling them back as they queued up to take their turn. It was exactly what I had hoped for: a positive interaction with his peers.

I never mentioned my request again to the boys, but things rapidly changed. As the weeks progressed, I watched in awe as Ramell stepped up to make sure Justin was always included. He invited Justin to play blocks with him, sit next to him in circle time, and play together on the playground. One day I watched him suggest he and Justin go play on the swings. This is something Justin would not have done on his own. They stayed on the swings a long time, and then I rang the bell for my class to line up and go inside. As the two boys walked by me to get a drink, I overheard Ramell say to Justin, "Let's do it again tomorrow."

Because of his charisma and kind nature, Ramell was well liked by everyone in class. So, it was a bit of a shock to the others when he began patting a chair at lunchtime and saying, "Justin, sit by me." Justin would go over and sit down. Ramell would casually say to the table, "Justin and me, we're friends."

And Justin would repeat, "Yeah, we're friends."

The other children listened and watched the two them closely. They were keenly aware of their growing friendship and the implicit message from Ramell was, "Justin *deserves* our friendship." His loving nature made it natural for him to hug classmates hello and goodbye at drop off and pick up, and I noticed without fail, he always made sure to give Justin his hugs.

As winter turned to spring, other children who had never played with Justin began inviting him to ride bikes or look at books with them. As Justin was able to practice his social skills and bathe in the acceptance of his peers, his confidence soared. His attitude also got much better towards me and the other teacher. Instead of telling us no when we asked him to do something, he would comply right away. As time went on, I watched Justin walk into class smiling and talking, instead of shuffling his feet and acting lethargic. I saw happiness on his face instead of a blank stare. His apathy was gone.

As if all of this wasn't enough, Ramell's friendship with Justin was having a noticeable effect on his immediate family. The other teacher and I saw a transformation in the relationship between Justin and his parents. During the first couple months at drop off and pick up, we didn't see much affection between Justin and his parents and there was very little conversation. As if by magic, it all started changing. I would see Justin holding his dad's hand when they came in together and Justin hugging his dad goodbye every day at drop off, doing exactly what Ramell had modeled for him. His dad started giving Justin a kiss on the forehead every day before he left.

I noticed the biggest change with Justin's mom. The first few months he was enrolled, she would walk in at pick up time and tell him to hurry up and get his things. She had never seemed interested in hearing about his day or looking at any of the artwork he always wanted to show her. When they would leave my classroom, she would walk ten feet ahead of him and yell back at him to hurry up. The other teachers and I watched this day in and day out, feeling a lot of sympathy for Justin.

I do believe in miracles, because in a few short months, I saw a huge shift in his mom's demeanor and attitude. I watched her come in at pick up time and *sit down with him* at the table where he and his classmates were drawing. She no longer acted in a hurry, and began asking him to tell her about his drawing. The picture was always the same: Justin in the middle, along with his mom and dad on either side of him. (His parents were separated) She also became friendlier towards me and we began chatting after class about her older adult children, her job, and Justin. For our end of the year party, she asked me what she could contribute, which I wouldn't have predicted four months earlier, when she barely spoke to me or the other teacher. Things were changing and it was all for the better.

What was Ramell's magic? It was so simple: love. His love for Justin helped his friend open up and express his love and affection for his parents. Justin learned many things through his friendship with Ramell, but the most important thing was that he saw himself as *worthy of friendship and love*. I asked his mom near the end of the school year if she had seen a change in Justin at home. She said, "Oh yeah, he talks all the time now; I can't get him to shut up." She made it sound like a bad thing, but I knew it was another sign that he had come out of his shell and he would have the skills to make friends in kindergarten. Although I have taught hundreds of students, Justin's story stands out in my mind as the biggest metamorphosis I have ever seen in a child.

Ramell, just four years old, is an old soul who intuitively knew this was a situation where he could help Justin. He modeled unconditional love, acceptance, and kindness to Justin and the whole class. You wouldn't imagine a young child could be such a loving teacher, yet he was. I always believed there were wise souls among us, and Ramell is one of them. In three months, he transformed another person's life. How many of us have done that? This remarkable child with so much love to give is already a bright light. It's easy to forget that by giving acceptance and love to others, we can literally change lives. Ramell was also my teacher, reminding me that *all of us* can make a difference and we should never underestimate what children can do to heal the world.

Ramell's mom shared an interesting story. I was talking with her one day and telling her how much he was helping another child in my class. I told her I had never seen a child with so much compassion and selflessness.

She smiled and said, "There were two different occasions when I was pregnant with him and a stranger came up to me and said, 'I want to tell you, I believe this child is going to be a huge blessing in your life.'" I smiled. Spirit was at work relaying messages and now I was telling her the same message again.

Ramell's dad is a successful rapper and songwriter who gigs all over the country. I've listened to some of his songs on YouTube and a lot of his material is adult themed, like a lot of rap music. We were talking one day after school and I told him, "You need to write a song about Ramell and the amazing person he is." His dad smiled and said, "Yeah, you're right!" I hope he does someday. He has a child whose love for others is inspirational and worth talking and rapping about. Ramell, with his beautiful light, will continue doing wonderful things to heal our world.

I want all children to feel loved, happy, and know they are capable of achieving anything. **Our message is simple: we believe in them.** They are our future—our better world starts with them.

Children are helping to heal the world.

Chapter 6: It's a Gift to Give and Receive

Drawing by Mia Jaraba

Is there anyone who doesn't like presents? As children, we are given presents for birthdays, holidays, and celebrations. Presents are the icing on the cake; the exclamation point that says, "This day is special." I still remember what I received for Christmas when I was eight years old, and you probably have some special presents that stand out from your childhood. Regardless of our age, gifts make us feel special, appreciated, and loved. As a teacher, I have been given many gifts from parents wanting to show their appreciation: handmade earrings, coffee cups, chocolates, candles, and other heartwarming gifts.

I've worked with children for many years, and once in an afterschool program, we made cool necklaces from colored clay that we rolled out and then cut and baked. When we finished, they looked like a piece of candy on a string and the kids loved them. Because they were so unusual, I would often get asked about them whenever I wore one. I've always kept a journal and while reading one last summer, I found this entry from August 15th, 2004.

While in the Detroit airport, I met a tomboy girl and she was admiring my necklace in the bathroom. She said, "I like your necklace—what's it made of?" I explained to her it was made from clay. We chatted briefly and then I took it off and gave it to her. I knew she would enjoy wearing it. A few minutes later she spotted me at one of the gates. She rushed up and gave me a big hug. "Thank you!" she said, "I wish I could make you a bracelet! Where are you going?" "San Francisco," I replied. She said, "Oh, I'm going to Grand Rapids." She was a very cute and appreciative little girl. I felt really good for making her day.

I know when I get the urge to do something for a stranger; it's Spirit talking to me. *The more we hear Spirit and act on it, the stronger that channel of communication becomes.* Don't be afraid to act on impulses that contribute to others' joy. In those situations, we are acting as a conduit for Spirit, bringing in positive energy. *We are shining our light.*

A Random Gift with a Big Message

For many years I taught in a community where the families were Hispanic immigrants and they often worked two jobs to make ends meet. I grew to admire their culture for its strong work ethic, commitment to family, and respect for education. One morning, one of my students and his eighteen-year-old sister came into the classroom. The boy was excited and smiling as he handed me a small glass vase with pretty stones and a candle inside. A lovely white artificial flower was attached at the top. I was a little surprised because it wasn't any special day. She said, "Andrew wanted to make this for you. He insisted I take him to the store yesterday to buy the materials so I could help him make it." Andrew, who was four years old, just stood there smiling.

So often children are unable to express themselves in words. His gift was his expression and it's message, though unspoken, was beautiful. I have cherished this handmade candleholder, and when I see it, I am reminded of why I love teaching. I have the privilege of spending time with children and helping them learn about the world and themselves. I was very impressed that his older sister helped him to act on his generosity. He has loving adults in his life who are guiding him to develop his true nature: thoughtful and generous.

How do we decide whom to give to? There is a verse from a song I learned as a child and it comes from the Bible, "Whatsoever you do to the least of my brothers, that you do unto me." I think of it every time I see homeless people begging in the streets when I visit San Francisco. I ask myself, "Should I give them something?" I've heard the argument that by giving them money I'm enabling them to stay on the streets. There are a lot of gray areas in life and this is one of them for me. I don't know if I'm enabling them, but I see they are the least of my brothers. Sometimes, I give to them and other times I don't. I know that when I give them money, I feel better as a human being. Maybe it's a salve for my guilt. When you see people with dirty hair, nails, and clothing, it's obvious they're not having an easy time in life. I know many of the homeless are dealing with mental illness and drug addiction. There are others living on the streets who are physically disabled as well as having these other issues. Some have chosen to live on the street while others have nowhere else to go.

For many homeless people, life is a daily struggle of survival. When I remember that I have emotional and financial stability and a family who cares about me, it's hard seeing people who have so little. I had a mother who was kind and loving. My parents were responsible and made sure we were always safe, and our needs were met. Many people didn't get that kind of love and care growing up. There are so many people in the world today who are "the least of my brothers," it can be overwhelming to think about. We can't save everyone we meet but we can send them loving thoughts and we can be kind. If we want to give them something, they are almost always appreciative of the gesture. I gave a guy $2.00 the other day at a stoplight in San Francisco. He smiled and said, "Thank you, sweetheart!" I noticed that most of his teeth were missing. I didn't expect his friendly reply and it really shocked me. It hit me that there was a time in this guy's life when he had a sweetheart, as well as family, friends, and very likely a stable life. It made me think about what he must have been through to end up panhandling on the streets. That is no life for anyone

Generous People

I grew up in a very large family and there were years when my parents struggled financially, but my siblings and I were able to participate in extracurricular activities, including Boy Scouts and Girl Scouts. Many of the girls in my class were also in Girl Scouts, and every Wednesday after school, we met in the gymnasium for our troop meeting. We played games, had snacks, and planned events. Every spring we sold Girl Scout cookies to raise money for field trips, parties, and campouts. None of this could have happened without our troop leaders—women who volunteered so much of their time and energy to Girl Scouts. Often in life, we don't appreciate someone or something till long afterwards. I wish I could go back in time and tell them how much it meant to me. Their generosity gave us something priceless: wonderful childhood memories. I give unending thanks to my troop leaders over the years: Jeanette Marossy, Mary Buttleman, Maryann Woodruff, and Polly Balenci.

I also went to Girl Scout camp for three summers on a scholarship, which they called camperships. My parents could not have afforded to send me to camp without financial assistance from the Girl Scout council. Attending Girl Scout camp was one of many positive experiences in my childhood. I made friends, went on slush hikes around a lake, took swimming lessons, performed in skits, cooked over a fire, and once again, I was around caring adults who were kind and helped me gain confidence in myself. I wasn't one of the three little girls in my family; I was Marilyn. I'm very grateful to the generous people whose donations gave me the fond memories of Girl Scout camp that I cherish to this day.

Is it Better to Give or Receive?

As a child I couldn't imagine that giving would be better than receiving. When I began volunteering as a tutor I discovered how rewarding it was to give back to others. I began working with fourth graders who were behind in math and had not learned their multiplication tables. As we met every week, I saw their sense of accomplishment soar as they made steady progress. They were very motivated because they didn't like being behind their peers in school. I worked with a fifth grader who also needed help with her multiplication tables. She had learned some, but nothing past the fives. Her teacher didn't want her to miss her class time, so Destiny would forfeit her recess twice a week to practice with me. Within six weeks she had mastered all of them. Even though the kids didn't express it verbally, it was clear from their smiles and hugs they were very grateful and appreciative for the time I spent tutoring them. Helping others touches us because it allows us to experience the joy of being the giver. Some people have financial resources to share, while others have intangible things like love, support, and time. Any gift, big or small, has the power to change someone's life.

Do We Accept the Gift?

People are generous for many different reasons. Their motives can run the gamut from being controlling and self-aggrandizing to altruistic and humanitarian. Sometimes, we don't know someone's motives for giving and we feel uncomfortable when they offer something, so we say no reflexively. If we are truly uncomfortable with them or their gift, we should say no thanks. But sometimes we say no without thinking or because we are embarrassed to take help from someone. When we say no for those reasons, we are rejecting the gift and the giver. The situation ends up being a disappointment for someone trying to do something nice, and we have lost out too.

One time, I went up to Lake Tahoe with a group of eight co-workers for the weekend. We rented a cabin and after dinner we decided to go to the casino to see if we could win some money. We arrived at the casino and split up, looking for the slot machine or table where we hoped we could win our fortune. I wandered around wishing I knew how to play something other than slot machines. I walked up to a craps table and began watching. Shortly thereafter, I struck up a conversation with a man playing at the table. We started chatting and I found out he was a writer for Sports Illustrated. He told me he was in town to cover a golf tournament that weekend. He said, "Why don't you hang out with me and I'll teach you how to play craps. Whatever we win I'll share with you." I didn't take him seriously, but I wanted to learn the game, so I agreed.

He began betting and explaining a few things about the game. I listened and studied the table, thinking it looked like hieroglyphics. I pretended to understand what he was saying, but honestly, I found it very confusing! The table started out quiet but after awhile, it got on a hot streak. It seemed like almost everyone was winning, and all of us at the table got very loud as the energy escalated. When people are screaming with excitement, it attracts a lot of other gamblers, and the crowd swelled around the table. Soon, everyone at the table was smiling and high fiving each other like we were best friends, and twenty minutes later we were up $150.00. When you see those chips stacking up in front of you, it's an adrenaline rush; it always feels good to be a winner! With the hot streak over, it was time to cash out. After the cashier gave him the money, he turned to give me half of the split: $75.00. He said, "You were my good luck charm; here's your share!"

I said, "Oh no, you keep the money!"

He offered again and I continued to refuse taking it. All right, I could have used the money. I was working for a nonprofit at the time and was not making all that much. I look back now and think, "Why didn't I take the money? He offered it!" You might be thinking, "Oh, there were strings attached," but that was not the case. It was my pride, pure and simple. He was a successful man and I didn't want him to think I needed the money. We live and learn as we go through life. If a situation seems fine to accept a gift, be in the moment, say thanks and enjoy whatever gift comes your way! It's a blessing to give and to receive.

Giving, receiving, and sharing is healing the world.

Chapter 7: Love and Compassion

"You, yourself, as much as anybody in the entire universe, deserves your love and affection." –*Buddha*

What is your story? What do you tell yourself and others about your life and your beliefs? Do you believe you deserve good things like love, friendship, prosperity, and peace? The book and the movie *The Secret* tell us that we only need to practice the Law of Attraction to attract these things into our lives. It says we attract to us whatever we think about. However, to bring our hopes and dreams to fruition, we must also feel we *deserve* it.

It seems we don't always believe we are deserving of all that we want. Whenever we have conflicting thoughts about something, we are effectively sabotaging our wish to bring it into our lives. That is why cultivating compassion is so important: we want to overcome, forgive, and heal any negative feelings we're harboring towards ourselves. Releasing negative thoughts clears the way for us to create those things we desire, and once we show compassion towards ourselves, it becomes much easier to offer compassion to others.

Compassion is a gift because it has the power to heal. Sometimes we will be the giver and other times the recipient. As we go through life, we begin to see the patterns and ebb and flow of how things work. This is why many people over forty often talk about how much easier life is—we learn to love and accept ourselves and take the pressure off. It is impossible to be judgmental and compassionate simultaneously. Which would you rather be? Which one would you rather receive?

We've all experienced disappointments and failures that we'd like to forget. Some people have been through emotional warfare in their childhoods. Others are still fighting emotional battles in their lives. One thing is certain; none of us escape the feeling that we've made mistakes that have negatively affected our lives. I've heard many people say, "If I had it to do over again, I would do things differently." None of us can go back, but we can go forward with the knowledge of what we've learned in those situations. The truth is: we learn the most when there is a challenge or adversity to overcome. No matter what has happened in the past, we must have compassion and forgive ourselves for anything we've done or haven't done or mistakes we've made. It will be impossible to create the life we want as long as we hang on to regret and blame. We are all here to learn, love, and grow as spiritual beings.

Our Path in Life

Most of us have had times in our lives when things were going along great and then our partner breaks up with us, we get a layoff notice, or we total our car on an afternoon outing. I recently did this with my car, so I know how it feels. Suddenly our peace of mind is gone. Our life feels out of control because we feel we didn't create these problems. (At least not on purpose!) We also know these problems can't be fixed overnight and this creates a lot of anxiety. We can't pretend our problems don't exist, *but we can choose* how we react to those events. It will be much easier if we can adopt a positive attitude. What that really means is we have faith that although things are crappy right now, they will get better. We just have to hang in there for the time being.

We know our thoughts affect everything: our energy, our mental and physical health, our outlook, and the degree to which we experience happiness. Sometimes when our life is upended, it's hard to remember that it's temporary. With life experience, we begin to see that problems have a way of working themselves out. We want smooth sailing all the time but that is not the way life works—for anyone. Even people who we perceive as "having it all" have their emotional ups and downs in life. For many, it is their faith in God or Spirit that keeps them going when the road gets rough. For others it's the knowledge that what goes down must come up.

The Road Gets Rough

I grew up on a beautiful eighty-acre farm in western Michigan. We were very lucky to have animals on our farm: three horses, cows, pigs, chickens, ducks, cats, and a wonderful dog named Bootsie. There were nine children in my family; three boys who were the oldest, then six girls in succession. I was number seven in the lineup and was often grouped with my two younger sisters. The other family members often referred to us as the three little girls.

On December 22, 1968, my parents returned home from a Christmas party around 1:00 a.m. When they walked in the house, there was a bitter, acrid haze of smoke in the air. Everyone one was awake, and my oldest brother Bob told my dad that he had checked the furnace and it was out. My dad touched a wall on the first floor, and it felt hot. He picked up a hammer and started breaking a hole in the wall, perhaps a foot across, between the kitchen and the upstairs stairway. Looking into the hole, he could see burning embers falling down through it. This meant that the fire was already burning in the upper part of the house. He told my brothers, "The house is gone—get out whatever you can."

Taking the High Road

My parents had been gone all evening at DuPont de Nemours annual Christmas party, and my oldest brother Bob, was out drinking with his friends. After watching the movie, *White Christmas*, everyone in the house had gone to bed. My sister Pat had woken up an hour later to a smoke-filled house and awakened my brother Jim, who was sixteen. He had gone down to the basement and checked on the furnace and he put it out, thinking the furnace was causing the smoke. My oldest brother Bob was seventeen and a senior in high school. He arrived home about thirty minutes before my parents. Walking into the house, Bob quickly began searching for a fire extinguisher. He found one on a ledge, going down the basement steps, but it was so old, it barely worked. Then he went down the basement and also checked on the furnace. The house was built in

1909 and we were still using the original coal furnace. He saw the draft was open, so he closed it. Then he noticed the pipe than ran from the furnace to the chimney. It was glowing orange, something he had never seen before. This was a red flag and he knew it meant the fire in the furnace had been extremely hot. He sprayed what he could from the extinguisher into the furnace to make sure it was out. Thinking he had solved the problem, he did not call the fire department. It didn't occur to him that the intense heat had started a fire somewhere he couldn't see: in the walls of the house. Probably no one would have suspected that, but the smoke was a clue that something was burning. It wasn't until my dad came home that the fire department was called.

As the story was retold later, my father never blamed anyone for what happened that night, although it would have been easy to do. Everyone knows you should call the fire department when you suspect a fire. Because of the unusual way in which the fire spread through the walls of the house, it might have burned down anyway. It would have been a tricky fire to put out. Because we lived eight miles from the town of Shelby and it was the middle of the night, it seemed like it took the fire department awhile to arrive, but considering they were all volunteers and home sleeping in bed, they got there relatively fast.

The Sky Lights Up in December

Before my parents arrived home, Bob had taken all six girls and put us in the car, which was parked in the driveway. I was six years old at the time, and my youngest sister was two years old. We were all wearing our winter coats over our pajamas. We sat out there watching as people began coming and going. I don't think any of us were crying; we all were in a state of shock at what was happening. Bob had put our dog in the car with us. When my parents arrived, they moved the car in front of our house. Soon afterwards, someone drove us to a neighbor's house where we spent the night.

The fire was in the walls and spreading throughout the house. My dad called the fire department and my mom quickly called her sister and some neighbors to come over and help get out whatever belongings could be saved. Because it was a slow burning fire in the walls, they were able to access the first floor while waiting for the fire department to arrive. The fire chief even allowed them to continue moving things out after they started pouring water up on the roof, which had now collapsed in places.

You can't believe how many belongings those good men carried out that night. They saved my mom's bedroom furniture, a couch, lamps, end tables, a kitchen table set, a dining room set, desks, rifles, and some men carried out a full-sized freezer full of food. It must have weighed several hundred pounds. It was all carried outside to our frozen cherry orchard or driven up into the upper barn by my uncle Doug, who had the good sense to bring his truck that night.

My brother Gary, who was thirteen years old, woke up in such a rush that he forgot to put on his shoes and his glasses. His bedroom was upstairs and once we all came down, no one was allowed to go back up. He was wearing only socks on his feet and was somewhat blind as all the chaos unfolded that night. As he was helping carry things out, he grabbed two things off our Christmas tree. One was a plastic angel that sat on top and lit up. The other was an ornament that he shoved into his pocket. It was a little porcelain elf wearing skis and smiling merrily.

In the Christmases that followed, the angel and the rosy-cheeked porcelain elf sparked many family conversations of our recollections from that night. They became symbolic of our old house and all the good memories from our childhood spent there. It's also bittersweet to see them hanging on the Christmas tree, because they are reminders of all the drama from that night and the hardship that followed. Although quite a bit was hauled out from the downstairs, nothing was saved from upstairs. In the attic, my mom had stored a lot of memorabilia: photograph albums, her wedding dress, and a beautiful cedar chest, which was a wedding gift. There were other family heirlooms as well.

The fire fighters worked hard to save our house on that moonless night, but by 3:00 a.m. the fire was raging, and the house was declared a total loss. My dad didn't leave the property till morning. He wanted to make sure the whole house completely burned so there would be no trouble from the insurance company regarding the claim. My brother Jim also stayed till the end to watch it burn. Because of all the chaos and confusion, Jim wasn't sure where the other family members had gone to spend the night. Two girls from his high school had been there watching the fire, and they kept him company till morning. Our family of eleven was now homeless.

My dad told the story that the next day he and my mom returned to the property. All that remained was a cement foundation, a metal part from a vacuum cleaner, and some warped marbles that has survived the intense heat. My mom began crying as she thought about everything she'd lost: her childhood home, countless possessions, and all of her photo albums stored in the attic. My dad said, "Let's be glad we're not going to a funeral in three days." It may have sounded a little harsh, but he was trying to keep things in perspective, and he was right; our family was very lucky no one was hurt or had died in the fire.

There was an article in the local newspaper a few days after the fire, detailing our family's plight. The headline read, "Home Fire Ruins Christmas for Family of Eleven." Once word got out, the donations poured in. Because we had nine children, people donated countless boxes of clothing as well as many other things. When we look at family photos taken in 1969, we are all wearing clothing from donations we'd received. We were starting over and when you have nothing, you appreciate everything. From my mom's teal blue Easter suit, to our swimsuits worn that summer, and our winter coats that fall, my family was in recovery mode. My parents were so appreciative that people had cared enough to help us. Those boxes of clothes and other items were stored at a friend's house while we lived in a trailer, and then were moved to the basement of our new house when we moved in. My family used many of those donations in the years after the fire.

Generosity can warm the coldest heart, heal the sad and broken, and bring light to dark places. To a family who lost so much in a house fire, the generosity shown us was something that we've never forgotten.

The House is Gone

Our family began the New Year in a way none of us could have imagined: we left a large four-bedroom, two-story house and moved into a singlewide trailer that was under 500 square feet. It had two small bedrooms, one bath, and a living room and kitchen combined. My siblings and I ranged in age from two to seventeen years old. My three oldest brothers who were teenagers at the time, had to sleep in an old school bus that had been converted into a hunting bus. We had borrowed it from a neighbor, and it was parked behind the trailer about thirty feet back. I remember going in it and thinking how bare it looked. I couldn't even imagine sleeping in there. There were two sets of rusty bunk beds located in the back of the bus. There was no insulation and only a small heater inside.

Michigan in the dead of winter can be brutally cold. Nights can get down to zero Fahrenheit, and the winter of 1969 was a hard winter. My brother Gary said there were some mornings when his shoes were *frozen to the floor of the bus.*

We still had animals on our farm, which was located about a mile away from the trailer. Luckily for us, the fire had not damaged our barn at all. My three brothers had to go back to our property twice a day to feed the animals. It snowed nonstop that winter, and the car was constantly getting stuck in the snow. They had to deal with putting chains on the car and pushing themselves out more times than they cared to remember. Sometimes, the snow was so deep, they had to park the car and walk in from the main road. Once in the driveway, they would walk past a big hole in the ground on the way to the barn. Only fragments of the foundation remained. It was a dismal sight. My poor brothers endured a lot that winter. My parents also experienced an inordinate amount of stress in their lives that year. Looking back, I never remember hearing my parents complain or argue while we lived in the trailer. If they did, it was not in front of us.

We lived in the trailer from January to August of that year. To get out of that tiny space, my mom would take us on Saturdays to visit the local library and then to the Shelby Roller Rink. It cost $1.00 to rent skates and the place was packed with children every Saturday. My mom would drop my sisters and I off and go visit her cousin who lived nearby. It was a lot of fun because it was a large venue with music blaring and we were free to roam around inside, eat, hang out with other kids, and be as loud as we wanted. It was a great respite from our tiny trailer.

Life carried on and as winter turned to spring, we could play outside more and that made it easier on everyone in the family. Our mom did her best to keep things normal for us with birthday cakes and visits from the tooth fairy. My oldest brother Bob graduated from high school in May of 1969 and my mom planned a big graduation party for him at our church. Over the summer, work on the new house went into high gear, and finally in August, it was time to say goodbye to trailer life. I don't have any bad memories of living there, although we were packed in like sardines. That is a testament to my parents, but especially my mom who never complained about living in a house the size of a cracker box for eight months that year.

The New House

All spring and summer, my parents, older siblings, and some dedicated relatives and friends worked to build our new house with the help of two carpenters. My parents decided to rebuild in the same spot where the old house had been, and my dad and older brothers spent every free moment working on the house. My dad had the equivalent of two full-time jobs during those busy months. In August of 1969, after hundreds of hours of work, we moved into a beautiful house that wasn't finished inside, but we didn't care. We could look through the studs into the other bedrooms and no doors were hung yet. I remember running through the house giddy with excitement. It looked colossal compared to where we had been for the past eight months. My oldest sister Pat, who was thirteen, quickly nailed up a blanket as a makeshift door for her bedroom.

Time gives us perspective and the pain of any event lessens, regardless of the trauma at the time. I know my parents looked back on that year as the most stressful year of their lives. They were lucky though; besides a lot of faith, they had friends and relatives who were there for them. Some neighbors would stop by and help my dad after work and on weekends. They were good friends who listened, brainstormed, and offered much needed advice. They helped my dad with electrical wiring and many other tasks. They were very compassionate and understanding to my dad's plight of finishing the house as quickly as possible and on a limited budget. My parents later admitted that the house design was not perfect, and they wished they'd worked some of the floor plans differently. There is a learning curve to everything, and my parents and the builders made mistakes. However, they chose not to dwell on them. When we look at the big picture, smaller things don't matter.

I saw how my dad's friends did so much to help him get through in an extremely stressful time in his life. We can do the same for others when they are struggling in a bad situation. Showing others we care can do a lot to alleviate their stress and help them cope with their challenges.

Bending Like a Papyrus

Our path in life is fluid and meandering; nothing stays the same for long. If we can be flexible and go with the flow, our experiences will be easier, and we can enjoy the trip much more. During those dark periods in our life, we must keep faith and decide to forgive ourselves if we make mistakes. We have to bend without letting life break us.

The tough situations we work through are teaching us important lessons. It could be about love, forgiveness, trust, patience, or any number of things. Spirit brings us opportunities to grow, because on a soul level, we've asked for it. There is no growth when we are breezing through life. Sometimes the lessons are painful, even heart wrenching. If we hang in there until things get better, we will have learned something about life and about ourselves. These experiences are molding us into wiser, loving, and more compassionate people. Like a badge of honor well deserved, we'll take that wisdom with us for the rest of our lives.

When we show compassion, we are healing the world.

Chapter 8: Where is my Peace?

"A dream you dream alone is only a dream. A dream you dream together is reality." –*John Lennon*

Peace is a popular word. We know this based on how often people look it up (top 10% of all words) and its usage. We constantly see its image and hear people talking about it in our culture. Why? Because peace is what *everyone* desires, whether or not they are consciously aware of it. The definition of peace is: 1. A state of tranquility or quiet: 2. Freedom from disquieting or oppressive thoughts or emotions. 3. Harmony in personal relations.

Let's think about peace as it relates to us on a macro level (our planet) and a micro level (our lives.) We look around in the world and it appears we are a million light years away from achieving peace. Many people have given up on the dream of global peace in our lifetime. It may seem like an impossible task, but in reality, it's never too early or too late to affect change. I like the story of David and Goliath because against insurmountable odds,

David defeats and slays a giant with nothing but a slingshot. (According to the Old Testament and folklore) When we think about all the violence and hatred still going on in the world, it can feel like our Goliath. But what if we could make hate and violence disappear or at least recede? Would you be willing to build a small part (of a larger foundation) of peace for yourself, your children, and everyone else in the world? Because of the intangible thread connecting all of us on a soul level, the lovely, peaceful thoughts you and I create have the *power to heal hate and divisiveness.* Do you believe we can make a difference?

Envisioning Peace in Your Life

Where do we find something abstract like peace? It is something *we create*, and it always begins from within us and emanates outward through our energy. We cannot create anything *out there* (our external reality) until we can create it on the *inside* (in our minds and hearts).

We create with our thoughts, so a great way to start is a simple mantra, "Peace begins with me," and "I choose peace." Use one of these or create one that rings true for you. Mantras help us direct our focus on what we want, so say them often, silently or out loud. Thoughts expressed out loud are more powerful and give them a sense of realism. The repetition anchors them in our consciousness, allowing us to draw them into our lives. You can also say them with your partner, your children, and your friends. Why not? *"Thank you for the peace in my life/ in our lives."* If someone is getting on your last nerve, you can repeat to yourself, *"I choose peace, I chose peace."*

If this is what you want, lay it down front and center in your life. **Reflect on what peace means to you and think of ways you can express it every day in a word, a thought, or an action.** As John Lennon said, "Peace is not something you wish for; it's something you make, something you do, something you are, and something you give away." We're artists creating our dreams, but first we must have a vision. Can you see it in your mind? Believe in the power of your thoughts. John Lennon did. His incredible vision of peace, expressed in the song, *Imagine*, has been inspiring people all over the world for almost fifty years. He talks about imagining a world with no possessions, no greed, and a brotherhood of man. The chorus expresses his wish that our "world will be as one."

There are many ways we can imagine a better world. What vision do you want to create? What do you imagine differently for yourself or the world? I imagine a world filled with harmony, one with no fighting or wars. Thoughts are real and their energy is shaping our reality every minute of the day. Choose positive, loving, peaceful ones, and soon this *will be* your reality. It is the Law of Attraction—in action. We pray, believe, visualize, create, and we show gratitude for the good things in our lives. Like Lennon, we believe anything is possible.

Imagine has become an anthem for peace throughout the world. In December 1980 in his last interview with Rolling Stone, Lennon said, "We're not the first to say, 'imagine no countries' or 'give peace a chance', but we're carrying that torch, like the Olympic torch, passing it hand to hand, to each other, to each country, to each generation...and that's our job." Lennon planted some potent seeds (thoughts) of peace in our world consciousness, and they have been growing ever since. Jimmy Carter, in a conversation with NPR, said, "In many countries around the world—my wife and I have visited about 125 countries, you hear John Lennon's song 'Imagine' used almost equally with national anthems." The song's message continues to inspire those seeking peace, but it's also a call to action. Dreaming isn't enough—we want to create.

Laying the Framework in Our Lives

We are artists creating our dreams, and the right frame of mind is important. We can't be creative if chaotic and worrisome thoughts are distracting us. We must calm our minds to allow this process a chance to grow and thrive. We rarely create anything instantly—most things happen incrementally and over time. Have faith that you are planting the seeds for peace today for yourself and the world. With time and focus, you will stand on a rock-solid foundation of peace that is unbreakable. Your peace becomes a gift to everyone. Don't ever doubt that you are powerful, a creator, and a healer.

Here are some ideas to help you find peace.

1. Slow down. Slowing down allows us to notice the beauty surrounding us, and beauty is calming and peaceful. Go somewhere quiet and pretty by yourself and don't bring your phone with you. You can do this—everything will be fine. All of us have become so used to having our phone with us all the time, we feel lost or a little panicked if we don't have it. I hope you will leave it at home or in the car. If you are hearing notifications, you won't get the full effect of immersing yourself in the moment. If you have a quiet backyard or patio, sit down somewhere comfortable and close your eyes. Listen to what is going on around you. Breathe deeply and take yourself to a place you love or just be in the momen enjoy the feeling. It's easy to imagine peace when sounds or stillness surrounds us.

If you take a walk or a bike ride, go out in nature and breathe in slowly as you notice the magic in the surrounding beauty. Depending on the season, you may hear insects buzzing near the trees or bushes, see birds and butterflies floating by, or spot a deer at dusk. Sunrise or sunset is an especially beautiful and quiet time to be outside. If you you're outside at night, the canopy of stars is engulfing and peaceful. When I look up at the Big Dipper and the billions of stars, it reminds me that I don't have to be in such a hurry. Find a place that you can go that brings you peace and restores your equilibrium. It's easier to receive messages from Spirit when we're in a tranquil place because it allows us to enter the quiet spaces of our mind and listen without distraction.

2. Gratitude brings peace. Expressing gratitude reminds us of the good things in our lives. Many years ago, a spiritual guide gave me some advice. "Never forget to show gratitude for all that you have. Thank the wind, the rain, the heat, the moon, and the stars for shining. Thank the wind for blowing. The reason to do this is it puts you into oneness with everything around you. It puts you into the channel of all of creation. So be very thankful."

I was given this guiding mantra when I was twenty-six years old and I have used it ever since. It's great to remember when you are outside, day or night. It always brings me peace because it reminds me that our planet is beautiful and it's a gift to be here.

All of us have many things to be grateful for. If your children are healthy, be very thankful. Millions of families have sick children and do not have that blessing. If you have friends and family who love you and care about you, send a prayer of thanks. Many people in the world do not have family or friends they can count on. Even if you are struggling right now in your life, give thanks for any and all of the wonderful things that give your life meaning. We attract to us what we think about, so dwelling on the good and the positive is what we want to focus on every day.

3. Accept what is. We don't always get what we want in life. If I wanted to, I could dwell on the disappointments in my life and how I wished certain things had been different. I'm choosing not to do that. Instead, I choose to focus on the great people in my life and all the blessings I've been given. I didn't have children by choice. Sometimes I wonder, "How much have I missed out?" "Was that a mistake?" I don't know, but I choose to accept it and not dwell on the "what ifs" in life.

Are there things in your past that you have not forgiven of yourself or others? Were situations or people unfair to you? Most of us deal with these kinds of issues, and it's important to come to terms with them. At some point, we have to let go of any anger or disappointments and focus on the future, not the past. If you are struggling with this, pray for understanding and peace in forgiving others or yourself. Pray to be healed. There is a lot of peace of mind that comes from accepting our past—it gives us the chance to live in the present and enjoy our lives.

4. Acknowledge that our world is not perfect.
On any given day we might see the best and the worst that humanity has to offer. We hear stories of pure evil as well

as beautiful stories of loving souls; the bright lights here among us. Since we can choose to see the glass half full or half empty in life, I'm choosing to have my glass half full. I'm focusing on the good things happening in the world, like a man giving a homeless person a sandwich or a woman letting someone with a few items cut in front of her in line. It makes me very happy to be in the presence of thoughtful, caring people. They demonstrate that goodness exists, and I like being around people who are choosing kindness as the experience they want to share. Anyone demonstrating generosity reminds us that we can choose love at any moment in our lives and in turn, we can show this to others.

There are some dark souls here among us who create a lot of pain and suffering for innocent people. They don't have a bright light yet because they don't understand that when you hurt someone, you are also hurting yourself. Every time a person hurts a living thing, (human or animal) and acts with hatred, they are holding themselves back from moving forward on their path. Every one of us feels the effects of their destructiveness and acts of malice. I don't engage with people or situations that give me a bad feeling or where I feel harm might come to others or myself. It would be easy to feel anger or even hatred towards those dark souls who seem to enjoy others' misery, but that doesn't solve anything. Instead of bringing light to the situation, I would be bringing darkness too. So instead, I pray for them. You and I can pray they'll find Spirit and love soon, because love will *always* prevail over hate. That's why we must *consciously choose love.* No one is lost forever. Eventually we all learn that choosing the path of love is what we want, and it brings us the peace we're seeking. By accepting the duality of good and evil in the world, I have found peace.

5. Pray for guidance. Whether we call it praying or meditation, we are having a conversation with God/Spirit. All of us pray about different things and often it reflects where we are in our lives. We will never know what is in someone else's heart—only our own. In my twenties and thirties, I prayed for help when I was stressed at work or was struggling with a difficult relationship. I was hoping for a quick fix because I had no idea how to handle those situations. I didn't know it then, but that was naïve thinking. Now I understand those problems were in my life for a reason: there was a lesson to be learned. In some instances, it was to be assertive and stand up for myself. Other times, it was to forgive people who had hurt me. God/Spirit will present us with situations that help us grow on our spiritual path. Rather than asking for a magic bullet to solve my problems, *it would have been wiser to pray for insight and understanding.* Now, when I have a conversation with Spirit, I trust that everything is working in my favor and I don't worry about the details of how things will work out. If we are patient, our prayers are always answered in a way that serves us best. Pray for what you need and trust that God or Spirit is helping you *the moment you ask.*

I was on an airplane a few years ago and sat next to a nun from West Virginia. She was wearing a habit, which I rarely see anymore. Times have changed dramatically since the 1970s when it was commonplace to see nuns wearing them out in public. She and I chatted about various things and I shared that I was a teacher and a writer. I told her I wanted to write a message about love, peace, and hope. I asked if she had any spiritual insights to share. She said, "Give me a few minutes." She closed her eyes and after awhile she turned to me and said, *"We're all one...and, we're given messages when we're ready."* I smiled and thanked her. Messages, inspiration, and insight—they have a way of appearing when we're ready. Sometimes we think no one is listening because nothing seems to be happening. We must be patient and know that the minute we ask for anything including peace, the process has begun.

6. Visualize a better world. Terrorism has been around forever, but with our round-the-clock news coverage today, it seems so much worse than in the past. In the 1970s, airplanes were being hijacked, eleven Israeli athletes were kidnapped and killed by terrorists at the 1972 Olympics, and in 1979, terrorists murdered Prince Harry's great uncle, Lord Mountbatten and two other innocent people by planting a bomb in his fishing boat. Now, in the United States, we are experiencing a national crisis with so many mass shootings and polarized groups who are unwilling to work together to find a compromise.

There is a lot of fear and negative energy on our planet, rooted in ignorance, hatred, judgment, and the false belief that we are separate from each other. Being immersed in that low-level energy has a tendency to bring all of us down, which is why surrounding ourselves with other positive people is important. When you see someone being kind or loving, say hello and introduce yourself. We are powerful in numbers, and we want to build connections and friendships with others who are shining their light. To be successful in visualizing our better world, we must keep a positive attitude and surround ourselves with energy that matches ours.

There are days when the news is full of stories depicting violence, and it seems there is no way to stop it. No way to stop the killing, the craziness, and the hate floating around out there. But we can't give up hope that things *will get better*. It would be easy to be pessimistic and say, "I give up on this lost cause of world peace." There is something in me that won't allow myself to do that. I choose to have faith. I choose to believe things will get better, and I pray for this often. Even if there are waves of chaos around us, we can choose peaceful thoughts. We are in control of how we perceive our world and how we let negative things affect us. I'm not saying to ignore or deny evil that is present today. I'm saying *I choose not to dwell on it*. Instead, I focus on how I can help solve this problem in our world. Is there something you and I can do to make a difference? **Yes, we can visualize a better world.** We can pray for peace, and say uplifting and healing words like, "Imagine peace now," "God, grant us peace," and "Peace be with us." We can demonstrate peace through our actions. When we give someone a hug, a smile, and tell them we love them, we infuse them with loving, peaceful thoughts. When we forgive others and love unconditionally, we are peacemakers. All thoughts and actions rooted in love are creating a peaceful vibration that is touching everyone, because we are all connected by the mysterious, intangible thread that links our souls together.

Yoko Ono is an artist, singer, peace activist, and widow of John Lennon. She has created Imaginepeace.com, where you can read messages about peace, buy John's music, and read about different projects she is involved with promoting peace in the world. There is also a global map showing the location of everyone who has visited her website since 2010. Close to five million people have visited, and over two million are from the United States. There are currently 228 countries registered on the site. Any movement where a group wants to affect change on this scale typically starts out very slow—so slow that it seems like nothing is happening. Have faith that good things are happening, because every single day we are healing the world with our thoughts of peace.

Peace Grows Where it's Planted.

When we have peace resonating in our body and soul, it will show in our facial expressions, our voices, and our overall energy. Because we're all connected, our peaceful vibration will touch others and be guiding them on their path towards peace. *Every peaceful thought is adding to the collective group consciousness of peace in the world today.* If we are a large group praying for peace and visualizing it, how can it not appear? It all begins with our thoughts—*they are the key to changing the world.* I hope you'll join me in creating a better world, where we will all be as one.

Our peaceful thoughts are healing the world.

Chapter 9: Relationships

Some people seem to be very lucky. They grew up in families that were stable, loving, and everyone seems to get along. But guess what? They're a small minority. Many friends and acquaintances tell me about the craziness they grew up with in their household. By and large, most of us grew up with dysfunction, myself included, and some people can and do write books about what they've endured. If you feel your childhood was less than ideal well, you're in good company. Many people have family members they struggle to get along with today. It stems from countless things: difficult personalities, resentments leftover from childhood, imagined and real wrongs endured, drug and alcohol abuse, and more.

If you are one of those lucky few with no war stories to tell, you still have to deal with difficult coworkers, bosses, spouses, or friends on occasion. How do we cope without feeling like we're losing control?

Handling Challenges

Throughout our lives, we will be challenged many times to love and forgive others, and often we won't want to do either. Relationships are one of the toughest things we deal with in our lives. People hurt us, they take advantage, and many other things that upset our equilibrium and peace of mind. How can we stay positive around these difficult people, especially when they often bring out the worst in us?

Every situation is different and unique and so should our strategies be for handling them. **Developing coping strategies is one of the most beneficial things we can do to make our lives easier**. Many situations will be trial and error but with persistence, you will figure out the best way to deal with your issue. You may also decide that you're not going to make a big deal out of a particular situation and let it go.

Of the strategies listed below, <u>number one is the most important</u>. Through prayer you will be guided to use one of the other strategies, or you may come up with one of your own. You are a creative and powerful healer. Never underestimate yourself.

Strategies for dealing with challenging people or situations.

1. Pray that you will be guided to handle the situation in a way that is best for everyone involved. *Pray for a healing and peaceful resolution.*

2. Send love and pray for them. Pray they will find peace. (Never underestimate the power of loving, healing thoughts.) The Law of Cause and Effect in action.

3. Visualize a positive outcome. Picture the situation *as you would like it to be, and do it often*—several times a day or more.

4. Offer a kind gesture as a way to pave the road to a better relationship. People will often meet us halfway, but they won't initiate it. We will have to be the bigger person.

5. Take the high road, act friendly and forgive them, as difficult as this can be.

6. Ask advice from someone you trust who knows them or the situation and can share some insights you may not have considered.

7. Choose not to be in their presence or limit your time with them. I avoid people who are unhappy and don't have positive intentions.

Number seven's strategy may not seem loving or spiritually evolved. However, if someone is hurting us and is unwilling or unable to change, we have every right to love ourselves enough to limit our time with them. This is an emotionally healthy thing to do and no one should feel guilty about it.

There are also people who thrive on drama. I'm sure you've met them, and you may even be related to a few. Often there is a crisis or problem they will magnify to try to get others more upset. They may also gossip, lie, backstab, and complain. Drama is the complete opposite of harmony and as long as you are in the company of "drama queens" you will not be feeling much peace. It is in our self-interest to limit our time with dramatic people. They will suck the energy out of the room and steal our peace of mind. To walk our spiritual path and fulfill our missions, we need happy, peaceful environments. I may limit my time with dramatic or difficult people, but I try not to judge them. We are all on our own spiritual path and doing the best we can, based on our life experiences.

Often, we have no idea what people have been through in their lives and the suffering they may have endured. There are a lot of unhappy people in the world. We can send them love and pray they will be healed from their pain.

Facing Rejection

We all like to think we're unique, and from a genetic perspective we truly are. As humans though, we go through a lot of the same emotions and experiences as everyone else. If we're lucky, we all get to experience feeling truly loved during our lifetime. Most of us have also known happiness, sadness, frustration, embarrassment, envy, disappointment, and rejection.

Rejection is one that cuts deep. There are few phrases that strike fear or pain in an adult's heart more than, "I want to break up," or "I want a divorce." These words are emotionally devastating to hear. Sometimes these words are not even spoken; they're conveyed through a text, body language, or silence.

Dealing with rejection is one of the most painful things we deal with in life. Whether it's friends, coworkers, or relationships, being rejected creates a barrage of negative feelings we have all experienced. It can happen to us at any age and it often happens out of the blue. It especially hurts if we like the person and they are rejecting us for their own reasons, which may be unknown to us. It can make us doubt our lovability and self-worth. We've all been there, and it can turn our world upside down.

For children, the dagger to the heart is, "You're not my friend." With children it's tricky because the truth is; we all like some people more than others. That's just a fact. We want to teach children to be accepting of everyone, not just their friends. It's a balancing act we learn in life. When I tell my four-year-old students we need to be everyone's friend, I see they don't quite grasp it. To them, the kids they like to play with are their friends, and the other children are not. It's very black and white. I explain it this way, "We all have special friends we like to play with, but we can be friends with everyone. I remind them that when we say, "You're not my friend," it hurts another person and we want to be considerate of their feelings.

Sooner or later, all children feel the bitter sting of rejection and will come to us looking for comfort and a solution. It's a big concept, but we need to help children and teenagers understand that rejection is not as personal as it seems. We know that no matter how great we are, some people just won't like us. They may not like the way we look, our laugh, or a dozen other things. We are just not their cup of tea. That's okay because if you really think about it, there are plenty of people who are not our cup of tea either.

Finding Your People

Knowing this, we look for people who will appreciate and accept us, and we can teach our children to do the same. That's how you know you have a true friend. They know everything about you, and they accept you. You can be honest with them and they don't judge you. You can be feeling down and need to talk about something, and they will listen sympathetically. Friends are out there in the world for all of us. If you haven't found them yet, keep looking. Many people who join groups like a sports league, a quilting group, a mommy play date group, or a hobby club, soon find they have a community of friends. This is wonderful thing—people in our lives with a common interest who we can count as friends. I have a girlfriend who joined an antique car club with her husband. They met so many other couples in this club and formed deep friendships with them. Meet ups are another great place to meet new people—right off the bat you have something in common: table tennis, hiking, or wine tasting. I have found most people at meet ups very friendly. I first went to a tennis meet up three summers ago while on vacation in Michigan. I only go once a year, but when I arrive, the guys are so welcoming. They say, "Marilyn from California, you're back!" It's wonderful, and I always have a great time playing tennis with this friendly group of people.

Nowadays we're all very busy but investing time in relationships is so worthwhile. We plant those seeds of caring and invest time in getting to know people, and soon, we have cultivated close friendships. Find your special people and they will adore you, believe in you, and help you when you need it. Having close friends is one of the greatest blessings we have in our lives.

I moved to California when I was twenty-four years old and I have no family living here; most of them are in the Midwest. There were many years when I did not go home for the holidays, so having friends I could spend time with was very important for me. Some people have lost all their family, or they may have lost contact with them. Many people ultimately see their friends as their family. Raise the bar high and choose friends who have your best interest at heart. We all need caring people in our lives and good friends are priceless. Friendships make everything better, especially throughout the highs and the lows that all of us experience in life. And if you're human, you're going to have plenty of both—welcome to life on earth.

Being a Friend to Others

There are a lot of lonely people in the world, which is why reaching out to someone is such a wonderful thing to do. As humans, we all want and need that connection. There are many people who are socially awkward and don't have any close friends. They may be introverted by nature or have an emotional or intellectual disability that keeps them from making friends easily. We won't become friends with everyone we meet, but we can be friendly to them. These conversations could be with a coworker, neighbor, or someone sitting in the park or on the bus. When we take ten or twenty minutes to chat with someone, that positive interaction is helping them develop social skills and build their confidence. When we think about Ramell and the profound effect he had on Justin, we know that small gestures can have a huge impact. Ramell is the quintessential role model because he embodied unconditional love and gave the gift of friendship to someone who truly needed it: Justin.

Remember Those Who Need Extra Love

I feel older people need our attention and care, because they, along with children, and the most vulnerable among us. A few years ago, I went to a happy hour at a bar in downtown Sacramento, and a distinguished, elderly man sat down next to me. I noticed the staff had a friendly rapport with him and greeted him by name. He and I began chatting and we spent the next two hours in a great conversation. I learned that his family owned a big fruit farm cooperative on the Delta, south of Sacramento, and they had been in business since the 1940s.

We talked about many different things that evening, most of which I don't remember. But he shared a story that I do remember because it almost made him cry. He told me he and his brother had been partners in the family business and they had worked hard to build it into a very successful enterprise. He had not had children, but his brother had two children, a girl, and a boy named Mark. In 1967, at age four, Mark drowned in the family swimming pool on their country property. His voice became sad and he said, "Mark would come in and see me every day in my office. I loved it when he sat on my lap and we would talk about things. You know, my brother never got over losing him and neither did I." I listened intently and it dawned on me that Mark would have been only a year younger than myself. As he got ready to leave, he said, "This is a great day; I got to talk to a young person." I thought about his parting words for a long time afterwards.

Many people, especially the elderly, do not have enough quality time with friends or family to give them the love they need. If you have elderly relatives, please give them the gift of a phone call, a visit, and a great conversation. It costs nothing and will probably be the highlight of their day. There is no one who wouldn't benefit from our smile or a friendly conversation. You could live in a town with a population of five hundred, or a city with four million inhabitants—it doesn't matter. We are all powerful and influential in the world of our making.

The Healing Power of Love

When all of us begin reaching out with love and acceptance, many of the violent acts we see in our world will cease to exist. Why? *Because love solves everything.* Those three words are a great mantra to say because it puts us in the flow of loving energy. It's one of my favorites because of its simplicity and power. What if all of us believed "love solves everything?" What if that was the pervasive thought that drove all of our behavior? It's hard to wrap our heads around because that is not what we see in the world today. If we use our imagination, we see that the world would be kinder, gentler, and much more peaceful. It's a worthy goal and it starts with us, our thoughts, and a desire to create something better. There are so many ways we can show love. If you made a list, you could come up with 50, or even 500 ways to show your love. We begin healing the world by sharing our friendship.

Love and kindness through relationships are

healing the world.

Chapter 10: Guiding Our Children

After teaching for many years, I've realized that helping my students become self-sufficient is just as important as academics and social emotional well-being. In preschool we talk a lot about modeling because it is such a great way to teach someone. As adults, we model behavior all day long for children. We model hatred or tolerance, grudge holding or forgiveness, and rudeness or patience. Whether you are a parent, grandparent, coach, aunt, uncle, or neighbor, we have countless opportunities to teach children every day. They will subconsciously adopt the attitudes, mannerisms, and behaviors of the adults in their lives. We want to bring out the best in our children, so let's sow the seeds for success in them. Modeling and cultivating the following qualities will help our children cope with life's many complexities.

1. Be Flexible and Go With the Flow. Often children cause themselves a lot of grief because they cannot accept no for an answer. It's their way or the highway. Please don't give in and give your children everything they want. We all have to learn to bend in life, and that includes children. As adults, we know we will not always get our way. If we teach children to accept the outcome of events and respect our decisions, everything becomes easier, both for you and them. There is a lot of peace that comes from accepting what is and not resisting what we don't have control over. People who are flexible often have a lot more friends than those who are not. Flexibility is an important life skill, and we can model it and teach it early to children.

2. Develop Grit. Grit is showing tenacity—you don't give up. We need to teach kids to finish all their work: homework, chores, and projects given to them. Having a good work ethic is important to success in life. Teach them to finish what they're doing and to do good work. When we are in small groups in my classroom and practicing cutting or doing an art project, there are always a few children who want to rush through it. I tell them, "Slow down and do good work."

Please don't jump in and do everything for your children. Let them have responsibility and allow them to work independently. Let them make mistakes so they can learn from them. That's how we develop grit. Our world is rapidly changing, and they will be learning many new skills throughout their lives. Let's prepare our children for the future by instilling grit in them. Life is less stressful when we know we can cope with almost any situation because we've been allowed to practice working things out on our own. This is a perfect segue to number three.

3. Be a Problem Solver. Often in life, if we keep trying, we figure things out. We want children to have confidence in their ability to take care of themselves and not quit the minute something gets difficult. Don't baby them—let them struggle a bit when it comes to problem solving. It teaches them fortitude and perseverance. Encourage them use their intellect to solve real-life problems. One of the things you can do to promote this is when you are in a situation that requires a solution, ask your children, "How should we solve this?" Let them brainstorm with you and think of all the possibilities. You'll be surprised at how clever their answers are. I've had four-year-olds come up with solutions that some sixteen-year-olds may not have thought of.

4. Be a Helper. How many times have you been doing something, and you're stuck, and then someone comes up and shows you a short cut or offers a solution? Your problem is suddenly solved. We all need GRIT but sometimes we also need help. *The people who are the most beloved in the world are those willing to help others.* There is a reason why the colloquial term "Good Samaritan" is so well known. The story of the Good Samaritan took place a long time ago. It is a biblical story that demonstrates true brotherhood and kindness. We all want to believe that if we were robbed and left for dead, someone would stop and help us. We need to model for children that it's okay to take time to help others. When we show compassion towards others, we are showing an aspect of love that is healing the world, because compassion is a healing act. Some children are born with compassion like Ramell, but we can teach it to anyone. Here is the story of the Good Samaritan. It is from the book of Luke in the New Testament and it shows us what compassion is.

Jesus answered, "A certain man was going down from Jerusalem to Jericho, and he fell among robbers, who both stripped him and beat him, and departed, leaving him half dead. By chance, a certain priest was going down that way. When he saw him, he passed by on the other side. In the same way a Levite also, when he came to the place, and saw him, passed by on the other side. But a certain Samaritan, as he travelled, came where he was. When he saw him, he was moved with compassion, came to him, and bound up his wounds, pouring on oil and wine. He set him on his own animal, and brought him to an inn, and took care of him. On the next day, when he departed, he took out two denarii, and gave them to the host, and said to him, 'Take care of him. Whatever you spend beyond that, I will repay you when I return.' Now which of these three do you think seemed to be a neighbor to him who fell among the robbers?" He said, "He who showed mercy on him." Then Jesus said to him, "Go and do likewise." Luke 10:30–37

If you do any reading about history during this time period, you'll learn that the Jews and the Samaritans hated each other. There was long standing bad blood between them. Not only was the Samaritan helping a stranger, he was helping someone who was looked upon as his enemy. The Good Samaritan looked beyond prejudice and fear and treated the injured stranger like a beloved family member. It's no wonder the term "Good Samaritan" has been around for 2,000 years.

I am always encouraging my older students who are almost five years old, to help the younger ones, who are only three years old. The older child feels a sense of pride that they have the skills to help someone, and the younger child loves the interaction and attention from an older peer. It's a win-win on all sides because both children enjoy it and it fosters closeness and camaraderie. It's also teaching them an invaluable lesson: we can help others and others help us. Isn't that what life is about?

5. Sidestepping in Life. Sometimes, people are really annoying in life—they are loud, they won't stop talking, or they are in our space. Our ability to solve an issue has a lot to do with the circumstances happening in that moment. Many times, the easiest way to solve it is for us to remove ourselves from the situation. It took me a long time to figure that out. I could solve the problem just by moving. Move to the other side of the break room, move to the other side of the bus, or another seat in the movie theater. You could confront the person or people bothering you, but it could make the situation worse. That's not to say that discussing your issue calmly with someone wouldn't work. It may work like a charm. But if it fails to deliver the results you want, try sidestepping. More often than not, it does work.

When the kids in my class are complaining about someone bothering them, whether it's standing in the line or another child touching their Legos on the carpet, I tell them to create some space between themselves and the other person. In my class last year, I would take a group of boys to a bathroom and they would stand against the wall waiting for the others to finish. We would sing songs or talk while waiting, but invariably, one boy or another would complain that someone was bothering them. I had intervened countless times, asking the boys to use their words and work it out, yet the problem persisted. Finally, one day I said to the boy who was complaining, "Okay, move away from the line and come stand by me." The boy did so, and the issue was resolved. A few days later the exact same scenario happened again. The same boy, who was four years old, just moved out of the line and came over to hold my hand. He had learned a strategy that now could be used in other situations.

6. Before you Shatter, Ask for Help. As much as we want children to be flexible, have grit, be problem solvers, and be a helper; there are times in our lives when we NEED help. We must make sure kids know that if they cannot solve a problem, it's okay to ask for help. **We want them to ask for help.** Sometimes children do not want to disappoint the adults in their life, or they feel we won't understand what they're going through. *Please let your kids know you love them* **unconditionally,** and they can come to you if they're struggling with drugs, bullying, school related issues, rejection, or anything else. Suicide rates continue to soar among teenagers, and many kids and teens often don't talk to anyone about what is bothering them.

7. Encourage Children to Open Up. Emotional intelligence is knowing what you are feeling, being able to express those feelings, and having the ability to control or self-regulate your emotions. Many people believe possessing this skill is key to personal and professional success.

Encouraging children to share their feelings can start when they're very young—three and four years old. Sometimes at school, a few children don't want to participate in games like Duck, Duck, Goose. They have never done it before and it's a bit intimidating to them. I always ask my students, "Why don't you want to play?" Often, they cannot articulate it, but sometimes they'll say, "I'm scared." I'll tell them, "It's okay; when you are ready, you can join in." They sit and watch their friends playing the game and eventually they always join in. When we listen to and honor their feelings, children (and adults) feel understood and secure.

Some children find it easy to talk about their feelings, while others cannot express them at all. When I hold conferences with parents, I give my students a communication goal, "Express their feelings out loud." In preschool, we can begin asking children about their feelings and encouraging their expression through words. A great way to model this is for us to share our feelings with them. As adults, we need to make sure that our sharing is appropriate to the child's age level. Statements like, "I'm really happy when," or "I'm sad because," is showing them how we express our feelings, and it's tacitly giving them permission to do the same.

When something happens, good or bad, you can say to them, "How do you feel about that?" Give them a chance to think about it. If they don't have an answer, just let it go. You can then share with them how you feel about it. It takes time for some of us to process things, so they may not be able to answer for a while. With time, they will get in touch with their feelings, and when they are comfortable, they will start sharing. Regardless of how old your children are, you can begin doing this with them; it's never too late. It's a very important skill to learn and master, because people who never learn to express their feelings are at a much higher risk for depression and suicide.

8. It's Okay to Cry. We want children to grow up to be well-adjusted adults. This means they are comfortable expressing all of their feelings. When we are overwhelmed with sadness, most of us cry. It's a natural expression, and for many, crying is a cathartic release. Even if you're not comfortable with showing emotion yourself, I hope you will allow your children the opportunity to cry if they need to, and not ignore, dismiss, or berate them. Allowing them to express their feelings is strengthening their emotional intelligence, and this skill will help them cope with stress, now and later in life.

I had a girl in my class last year whose parents were going through a bitter divorce. As the year went on she began to show more and more signs of emotional distress. Leslie would come in teary eyed some days or just start crying at breakfast or lunch. It was upsetting her classmates to see her so distraught because they couldn't figure out why she was crying. She had a very hard time expressing any feelings, except through tears. I began to seat her next to me at breakfast and lunch so we could chat more easily. Slowly, she began opening up and sharing her feelings, "My mom and dad don't live together anymore," and "I miss my dad and my mom." I would listen quietly, and then remind her she had wonderful parents who loved her very much. They were doing a split custody arrangement, and as the youngest child, it was taking a big toll on her.

As the end of the school year approached, the babysitter told me her fifteen-year-old brother would call her a crybaby whenever he saw her crying, which I suspected was often. This was upsetting Leslie even more. I asked her to come over and sit by me. I held her hand, looked into her eyes and said, "You are not a crybaby. Everybody cries and it's okay to cry. Next time, tell your brother that it's okay. Miss Marilyn thinks it's okay, your mom thinks so, and so does Shari (the babysitter)." She just looked at me with her big brown eyes and said nothing. About two weeks later, a child began to cry in class. She immediately looked over at me and said, "He's not a crybaby. It's okay to cry because everybody cries sometimes." I nodded, smiling, "That's right; everybody cries sometimes."

We offered group counseling at my school for children who were going through or had been through a traumatic event in their lives. Some children have a lot to deal with at an early age: parents incarcerated or dealing with a drug problem, divorce, terminally sick parents, and more. I suggested the support group to Leslie's parents, and they agreed. It was a small group dynamic where they made fun crafts and created opportunities for the children to talk about their feelings in a relaxed setting. She never wanted to go, but when she returned she was always smiling, so it was a positive experience for her.

In the twelve months since she's left my classroom, Leslie and her mom have texted and sent pictures and video clips to keep in touch. Her mom shared that she was reading and doing very well in kindergarten. It's nice to see Leslie smiling and happy in the videos.

9. Violence in Our Children's Lives. We must protect children from seeing gratuitous violence as much as possible. In the scope of their lives, the time spent in childhood is brief. When children see and hear about bad things happening in the world, it scares them and causes worry. We know we can't protect them from everything, but think about what your child is exposed to in movies, television shows, video games, and conversations. I'm shocked at the violent video games some children are allowed to play. Why are four- and five-year-olds playing adult-themed games and watching horror and R-rated movies? Sex, violence, and adult language is something kids learn about early these days, but sheltering them from it, to the degree that you can, is a wonderful thing to do for your kids.

Watching a movie with disturbing images is not a good thing for children to see. I had a three-year-old student who came to school and she kept talking about a killer clown movie. She told me at lunch one day, "There's a clown in the movie and he's chasing people; it's not real, no, it's not real." Her eyes were big as she talked excitedly about the killer clown. Sharing the story with me was helping her process what she had seen, and she was also looking for reassurance that it wasn't real. It only takes a little effort to control the content kids are watching, or watch those movies later when the kids are asleep.

10. Children do Listen. In your home, kids hear everything! Children are fascinated with adult conversation and naturally want to hear everything you are talking about. Please protect your children from overhearing arguments. You would be surprised the stories children have told me. I've had children repeatedly tell me the story of a fight; "My daddy threw my mom's phone across the room and broke it; then she started crying." "Daddy and mommy were pushing each other and then he said, 'F- you.'" Another time, a four-year-old told me, "My sister called the cops on my mom again." I asked, "How old is your sister?" She said, "Thirteen." Please put your children first and don't fight in front of them. It pains children to see their parents upset and it creates a lot of insecurity in them. Please keep the name-calling and negativity away from the children, whether it's in a movie or the real-life drama in your household.

11. Co-parenting with Exes. Divorce/breaking up and the relationship that evolves with an ex afterwards can be an emotional landmine for many people. As someone famously said, "There is a fine line between love and hate." One of the most common offenses of parents who have split up is saying bad things to the kids about the other parent. I know most people would walk through fire before they would hurt their children, but because of their bitterness, anger, or feelings of betrayal, they unleash horrible things about the other parent. Those comments are devastating to children *at any age*. Please think about that the next time you are "just being honest" with your kids. It's hurting them more than you know, and it's something they will remember in twenty years with pain in their heart.

We can change our behavior whenever we want; it's a conscious choice we make. You can even share with your ex that for the benefit of your children's happiness, you are not going to "go there" anymore. You never know, by you taking the high road, they may decide to follow suite. We never know what works until we try. Regardless of what your ex does or doesn't do, you can keep it positive for your children. They will love you all the more for it. And don't be afraid to pray for a peaceful solution. We can plant the seeds for peace everywhere. "Let peace begin with me."

Guiding our children with love and wisdom

is healing the world.

Chapter 11: Who are the Invisible People in Your World?

Every day we see a lot of people when we go out in the world. Have you ever stopped and wondered who they are and what their story is? How about your neighbors? Do you ever stop and talk with them? Times have changed a lot since I was a kid in the 1970s. Back then most families only had one or two television sets and a radio, so people went outside and talked to their neighbors or called their friends on the phone to find out the local news and gossip. Technology has changed everything and impacted our lives in ways that has made our lives easier, but it's also created a lot of isolation among us. Whether it's teenage girls lying on the beach or couples and friends in restaurants, we now routinely ignore the people next to us as we use our smart phones to text, communicate on social media, and post pictures of ourselves. Have we turned into narcissists?

I was in Berlin, Germany in the summer of 2016, and after a long day of sightseeing, I would return back to my neighborhood and stop to have a beer at a local bar. Many establishments have outside tables on the sidewalk, so people sit in small groups with friends and have a drink. I noticed something very interesting. I almost never saw anyone on his or her smart phone or computer while at these bars. All the patrons were sitting and talking to their friends and completely focused on the conversation they were having. Of all the times I went, only once did I see a woman who was alone, working on a laptop. I was really impressed to see Berliners understood that being 100% present with people is a gift we give them. Texting and posting? It can wait.

It's so easy to stay in the safe zone in our lives. We visit our favorite restaurants, order the same things on the menu, and drive home the same way. Our schedules are dialed in and we like it that way. There is always tomorrow to go on that hike or take that dance class. Humans like predictability and that's not a problem, as long as we remember that as permanent as our life feels, *it's an illusion.* We know that today is all we have, even if we forget it sometimes. What if we were to start up a conversation with our neighbors or the lady in the park? What if we welcomed the new family to our school or to the neighborhood? How might that impact them and us?

Be my Neighbor

My sister and her husband live on a quiet street in Michigan named Flower Creek Road. There is a creek that runs through this area called Flower Creek. It is a wooded area with about fifteen houses on a dead-end street. As the crow flies, they are about a half-mile from Lake Michigan. It's a pretty location, and this is where I see fireflies when I'm walking at night. I always spot them clustered on the edge of the woods. Floating in the darkness as they communicate with each other, they remind me to slow down, be in the moment, and enjoy the beauty surrounding me.

Carol, my youngest sister, is very friendly, and so is her husband Paul. When they moved there several years ago, they started walking their dog in the evening. As they walked, they began talking to their neighbors and getting to know them. Many of them also had dogs, and we all know dog owners are kindred spirits. Over time, they began socializing and having potlucks together. Once they had a progressive dinner. That's when three families volunteer to host the other couples. As a group, they stroll through the neighborhood, visiting the different hosts. The first family serves the appetizers, the second one the entrée, and the last host, the dessert. Since this was a potluck, the hosts didn't have to prepare everything, just serve one dish and set their table!

As the friendships have grown, so has the number of gatherings. Now there are lots of parties: Carol hosts an annual New Year's Eve party, another neighbor does a summer hot dog roast, and another family hosts a summer ice cream social. Then there is Frank, who has a Sugar Shack. He has about one hundred fifty maple trees on his property that he taps for syrup. It's a side business of his family's. Every spring he delivers a jar of maple syrup to all of the neighbors. Another neighbor takes his golf cart in the summer and loads it with his extra vegetables, then drives around giving them away! They have created an atmosphere of kinship in their small corner of the world. As Gandhi said, "Be the change you want to see in the world." Carol and Paul wanted to have friends among neighbors, and they do.

From the Heart

When you develop genuine friendships, you know you can count on them in times of need. Carol developed a very close friendship with one of her neighbor's, Dee. She was a great friend; caring, easy to talk to, and always smiling. Dee shined her light effortlessly. One summer after not feeling well for several weeks, she went to the doctor. After running tests, her doctor had the difficult job of telling her she was much sicker than she knew: Dee had stage four pancreatic cancer. She had just graduated two months prior Summa Cum Laude with a bachelor's degree in theology and was planning to leave her career as a hospice nurse to become a chaplain for hospice patients. Instead she was given a different task: getting her life in order quickly and saying goodbye to her two adult children and everyone else she loved. Carol was faced with the heart-wrenching job of helping her get everything in order before Dee became too sick to handle it. Everyone was devastated by the news.

The neighbors of Flower Creek Road and Dee's family rallied and were all there for her in the five weeks before she passed. They quickly finished landscaping her back yard so she could sit outside and enjoy the view. A schedule was made, and they took turns bringing dinner every night for the relatives and caregivers who kept vigil at her house. My sister reassured Dee that she would adopt her dog, Odi. He was a good buddy to Carol's dog

Maddie, so it was an easy decision for Carol and Paul to make.

Dee was completely taken care of by caring relatives and neighbors, including her cousin Dave, a retired nurse who flew out from California to help care for her. When we reach out to people and befriend them, we never know how much that relationship will affect our lives. Dee lived a life of grace and kindness, and her friendship enriched Carol's life and the lives of everyone on Flower Creek Road. They will never forget Dee or her bright light.

When we have to say goodbye to someone we love, it can feel like an impossible task. When our heart is breaking, that is when we know we have truly loved. Here is a beautiful poem that was shared at the celebration of Dee's life.

A long time I have lived with you.

And now we must be going separately to be together.

Perhaps I will be the wind to blur your smooth waters

So that you do not see your face too much.

Perhaps I shall be the star to guide your uncertain wings

So that you have direction in the night.

Perhaps I shall be the fire to separate your thoughts

So that you do not give up.

Perhaps I shall be the rain to open up the earth

So that your seed may fall.

Perhaps I shall be the snow to let your blossoms sleep

So that you may bloom in spring.

Perhaps I shall be the stream to play a song on the rock

So that you are not alone.

Perhaps I shall be a new mountain so that you always

have a home.

–Nancy Wood

A New Day and a New Way

If we're not stepping outside our comfort zone, we're not growing in life. There is nothing inherently wrong with this except it's not challenging our soul's progression. To be fully alive we need to be in the flow of life, not on the sidelines. When you run an errand or are out in public, how often do you look at people and smile? Maybe say hello or good morning? I'm not talking about your favorite waitress, I mean a total stranger. We need to give ourselves a push to be open-minded in meeting people and trying new things. What might happen if we did? None of us knows how long we'll be here, but if fortune favors the brave, we can step out to new adventures and friendships with others. Showing interest in someone is a small gift that may touch him or her in a way you may never know. It may also touch us.

Positive Imprints

Sometimes we impact people and we have no idea anything has happened. For many years I've been a regular singer at a popular karaoke bar in San Francisco. A few years ago, I was there on a Sunday afternoon, which is one of my favorite times to go because there are a lot of regulars who stop by. This is the kind of place that is so friendly, it's easy to reconnect with old friends and to make new ones on any given day. I always joke that this place sits on a magical vortex because the vibe is so special. The truth is, it's always the people that make a place special. That day a young guy tapped me on the shoulder and said, "Hi, I remember you." I turned to look at him but I didn't recognize him. I searched my memory trying to recall if we had ever met, but he didn't look familiar. He continued," I was here a year ago and I sat over there." He pointed to a row of bar stools that overlooked the bar area. "I was here alone and I didn't know anyone. I looked down at you and you looked up and smiled. I never forgot that." I was taken aback and really didn't know what to say. This man was telling me that because I smiled at him, he remembered me a year later? Really? How could something so small have an impact on someone? He wanted to make sure I knew.

Spirit Whispers

I thought about this encounter later and had a small epiphany. Was it a coincidence that I was there a year later once again with this man? Even if we were together again at the same time and place, he could have easily chosen not to talk to me. After all, we were strangers. Yet he reached out to connect with me. Was it pure chance? In my mind, it was Spirit talking through him saying,

"Marilyn, when you are friendly and accepting of others—it's a good thing. Kindness *does* make a difference in the world." We never know the kind of impact we will have, but that day I was given a glimpse. We are all connected on a soul level by the mysterious, intangible thread. As we are living our lives, we will have many opportunities to step up and be the bright lights we came here to be.

Reaching Out

Sometimes we find ourselves alone at a party or a work function. Here's a typical scenario: the one person we know is totally engrossed in a conversation with someone else. We look around and feel bored. Instead of looking at our phone for the umpteenth time, what would happen if we struck up a conversation with a complete stranger? For those who take the risk, here are some potential outcomes:

1. You have a great conversation.
2. You make a friend.
3. One or both of you have a good time.
4. You learn something you never knew.
5. You end up cheering them up or vice versa and you leave in a better mood.
6. They give you sage advice. You can believe this is Spirit talking to you.

Listening to the Message

In 2000, I went to Esalen for a four-day retreat. Esalen is a retreat center situated near Big Sur, California, and it sits on a cliff overlooking the Pacific Ocean. People come from all over the world to experience the magic there, and the location is absolutely stunning. I had always heard it described as beautiful, spiritual, and a place to open your mind to new ideas. It was all that and more. I took some workshops while I was there, but there were also breaks throughout the day so I could chat with others, meditate, and relax. It was so peaceful being there; the energy felt completely different than the outside world. One thing that really helped me feel completely immersed in the retreat's vibe was the decision to leave my phone in the car for the entire four days. When you don't have a phone in your hand, you can really focus on what others are saying. I had so many great conversations with people who would just casually drop these epiphanies that I could ponder afterwards. I feel like I received many messages from Spirit while at Esalen. A few months later, I wrote in my journal, "I think my trip there was key to getting more in touch with my feelings. I'm so much more aware of how I am REALLY feeling about things. When do I feel uncomfortable? Saying "no" when I do. I only wish

I'd had that insight when I was eighteen." Esalen reminded me that relationships, and sometimes, even conversations have the power to change us in ways we never imagined. We only have to reach out and not be afraid. I wrote this poem while I was there.

"Grab the Brass Ring"

I am not in prison. I will never put myself there.

I am a prism, a vehicle for light to shine through me and out of me.

I can choose the roles I play: magician, muse, clown, healer, loving sister and artist.

That is how I will dance through life.

I will offer you my hand and my heart, knowing you will do the same.

I will be a feather floating and light, refusing to let anything bring me down.

I will be the lioness and scream at anyone who thinks of harming you.

I will be a pillow that you can rest on when you are weary.

I am the tall tree that will not be blown over by the cold wind.

I am the prism, reflecting your light back to you, so you can see your true beauty.

I will find the path that will take me to the place of creating the beautiful images that reside in my head.

I will take my vision and transform, inspire, and create.

When we reach out to others, we are healing the world.

Chapter 12: The Peaceful Revolution

It was pitch dark and the air was brisk on the morning of November 10th, 1989. I left a rustic youth hostel in Greece at 4:00 a.m., walking down a dirt road in complete silence with several other college-age travelers. Without any light pollution, the stars were shining brightly and filled the night sky. We walked for ten minutes into a small town where we waited at a bus stop for a van to take us to the airport in Athens. I was booked on a 6:30 a.m. flight headed back to New York. My six-week backpacking trip was over, and feeling road weary, I was very happy to be going home. I remember it was a smooth flight and a beautiful November day, looking out at the sky from my window seat. While drinking a lot of much needed coffee on the first leg to Frankfort, a flight attendant made a stunning announcement: "We have just received news that the Berlin Wall has fallen!" A shock wave reverberated through the cabin, as we all looked around at each other. How was that possible? Many of my fellow travelers were German, and the cabin was abuzz after the announcement. I remember feeling happy, knowing something momentous and wonderful had happened.

As an American living in the United States, I had always taken for granted that I could travel freely, speak my mind publicly, and vote my conscience, without ever feeling afraid to express my personal opinion or my political views. In many places around the world however, people have never had those freedoms, and living freely in a democracy is something they can only dream of. That was the case in East Germany till the day the wall fell.

Life in East Germany after World War II and continuing on till November 9th, 1989 was vastly different than life in West Germany and other democratic countries. The East German government was repressive and controlling; over two million East Germans had fled the country for their freedom between 1946–1961. To keep the other seventeen million from following, the East German government began building a wall along its border on August 13th, 1961, which eventually ran the full length of their country. With a physical barrier keeping them in and men patrolling the border 24/7, the citizens of East Germany felt like prisoners in their own country.

The German Democratic Republic (GDR) existed from 1949-1990, and was run as a satellite regime under the Soviet Union. Living under a communist power meant no religions were officially recognized, travel was greatly restricted, and citizens were not allowed to express any dissenting or negative views of the government. The Stasi, or Ministry for State Security, monitored citizens whom they considered suspicious, dangerous, or a flight risk. East German citizens were afraid to speak out or complain about anything, for fear of being harassed, arrested, or beaten.

The Stasi used informants to spy on others so they would know if someone was planning an uprising or trying to escape. An estimated 190,000 people were informants at any given time. Spying was one of the top priorities of the Stasi and spies were used everywhere. They planted microphones and hidden cameras in people's homes to gather audio and videotapes of conversations. There were informants planted in every apartment building and they monitored who visited people in their apartments and if they spent the night. Schools, universities, and hospitals were filled with informants, as were many other organizations and industrial plants. A large number of informants were people who worked with the public: teachers, nurses, doctors, janitors, and bus drivers. As Americans living in this kind of Orwellian world, it would feel like a nightmare. Can you imagine having to worry if neighbors, co-workers, or others are spying on you, day or night? It makes sense why so many people wanted to leave, and the fear and frustration felt by those forced to stay.

In 2012, the Stasi headquarters and their entire files were opened to the public for the first time. German citizens could now find out if they'd been spied on, what information had been collected, and who their informants were. When we hear the true stories of oppressive governments around the world and the lack of freedom their citizens have, we must give thanks for our great democracy in the United States.

Planting the Seeds

In the city of Leipzig, Germany, situated two hours south of Berlin, Reverend Christian Fuehrer, pastor of St. Nicolas church, decided to start a Monday evening prayer meeting in 1982. St. Nicolas is a magnificent 800-year-old church, and it is revered for its stunning architecture and beauty. In Germany, however, it's known for another reason: **it is the birthplace of the peaceful revolution**. This revolution for peace affected millions of lives and rewrote Germany's history. It restored to the people of eastern Germany what they'd been denied for forty years: their freedom.

Christian Fuehrer began the prayer meetings for peace on Monday evenings at the church, and in the beginning, there was not much interest in them. Feeling discouraged after a few years, he wondered if the meetings shouldn't be disbanded, but the regular attendees encouraged him, saying, "Let's continue, we don't want to give up." They continued on and in 1985, the pastor put out a sign reading, "All Are Welcome." This was loaded with symbolism, because the church was the only place people felt safe discussing things they could not talk about in public. Atheism was the official doctrine of the Communist party; however, churches were considered a sanctuary where people were protected. Having the meetings here gave people the courage to express their dissatisfaction with the government and their desire for change. More people began attending, and by the summer of 1989, the number had grown to hundreds.

The communist government was aware of the weekly meetings, and as they grew larger, tried to discourage people from attending. The attendees refused to be intimidated, and the weekly meetings continued.

There was good reason to fear the government. In 1989, there was no such thing as civil or human rights in East Germany. You could be arrested, interrogated, and held without cause. Leanna, a member of the group *Women for Peace* who helped organize the prayer meetings, recalled on the BBC Heart & Soul program how she had already been harassed by police and reflected on the anxiety the protesters experienced.

"I had lost custody of my children for a while and they even threatened to put my youngest daughter into a children's home. The official documents said I was unfit as a mother because I was involved in extremist groups."

Monday Demonstrations

During spring and summer of 1989, the number of people attending the prayer meetings grew steadily. Then, on Monday, September 4, 1989, peaceful demonstrations began spontaneously happening *after* the prayer meetings. Knowing the church supported their desire for a more democratic government and freedom to travel, people began putting aside their fears and gathering in the courtyard of St. Nicolas after every meeting. As word spread throughout Leipzig, more and more protesters came out every week to support the demonstrations. They became known as "the Monday demonstrations" and they began happening all over East Germany.

On October 7, 1989, the 40th anniversary of the German Democratic Republic, protesters took to the streets again for peaceful demonstrations in Leipzig and East Berlin. On that day, hundreds of protesters were arrested and beaten in front of the Nikolai Church in Leipzig, and in East Berlin in the Prenzlauer Berg district and at the Palace of the Republic. In Leipzig, an article appeared in the newspaper warning "the counter–revolution would be put down on October 9th with whatever means necessary."

On Monday evening, October 9th, 1989, the citizens of Leipzig gathered for another protest. This time was different: 8,000 armed riot police were also in the streets, waiting for the demonstrators and ready to squelch the demonstration. All day, people had been hearing rumors that violence would be used against the demonstrators. Machine guns were placed on bridges and there was a sense of foreboding in the air.

That night, it was standing room only inside St. Nicolas. The church holds 1,400 people and an estimated 2,000 attended the prayer meeting that night. A sign was placed outside saying, "Church closed due to overcrowding." Several other churches in the downtown area opened up and they were filled with people too. That night, the citizens of Leipzig prayed for peace, including many who had stayed home for fear of being beaten or shot. In church, the Beatitudes were read, including, the passage, **"Blessed are the peacemakers, for they shall be called children of God."**

When the people exited the churches after the meetings, they were met with an enormous crowd that had gathered outside to protest the government and their restrictive policies. An estimated 70,000 citizens filled the streets, the largest group protest since the wall had been built in 1961. Thousands of demonstrators carried candles, along with banners saying, "We are the people!" The enormous crowd began chanting, "We are the people," along with "No violence!" They marched around the city's Ring Road, and when they got to the State Building—Ministry for State Security (STASI), instead of vandalizing it, they left candles burning on the steps. Then the crowd marched on to Karl Marx square for a rally.

BBC's Diplomatic Editor Brian Hanrahan was there on assignment to get video of the demonstration and remembers,

"Around the city on that Monday night there was a palpable sense of menace. Riot police with shields were blocking the main roads; armed troops and militia were backed up in the side streets; hospitals were on standby for casualties; and inside the Stasi headquarters, I later learnt, they had pistols and rifles loaded with live ammunition pointing at the demonstrators as they passed by.

A massacre on the scale of Tiananmen Square was in the cards and only averted when the local communist leadership backed down. They ignored their orders from East Berlin to stop the march by any means necessary, and struck a deal with the protesters that they could go ahead provided the demonstration stayed peaceful. But it was all very last minute."

Do you think that was coincidence? *All things were working in their favor* that night. Their collective energy was powerful, and with peace in their hearts, they were changing the course of history. The government expected violence from the protesters that night, but there was none, only thousands of candles glowing in the darkness. Not one life was lost during this protest or the protests that later followed in Dresden, Berlin, and Plauen. These protests put tremendous pressure on the East German government to make changes, and exactly one month later the Berlin wall fell on November 9th, 1989.

As Pastor Fuehrer said later, "It's a miracle of biblical proportion that this revolution remained peaceful." What began as a prayer meeting with four people attending ultimately became 70,000 demanding their freedom peacefully. As it says in the Bible, Matthew 18:19-20, 'Wherever two or more are gathered in my name, there I am in the midst of them."

This is an inspirational story, yet few people outside Europe are familiar with it. So often, groups fighting for a cause resort to violence as the way to be heard. The story of the peaceful revolution in East Germany is one of faith, hope, and peace, but especially the latter. We know what was in the hearts of the people that night, because it showed up: PEACE. The Law of Attraction was at work in Leipzig. These people were not marching against oppression and tyranny, although they loathed it. They focused on what they wanted: Peace and freedom. The fall of the Berlin Wall happened for many reasons, but the people who witnessed these events believe it started in September 1982, when Pastor Christian began his prayer meetings for peace and invited others to join him. The people of former East Germany showed us nothing is impossible.

Blessed are the peacemakers for they will be called children of God.

Chapter 13: Making a Difference

"There are two ways of spreading light; to be the candle or the mirror that reflects it." *–Edith Wharton*

Sometimes it's easy to forget there are seven billion people on the planet, living in 24 time zones. Planet Earth is teeming with people, most of whom we will never meet. When we open our hearts and our minds we realize that all those people are just a different version of ourselves. We are all one, made by God and here living our lives in the best way we can. People who travel abroad learn that wherever you go, you'll find families who work hard, love their children, and love and serve God, regardless of their customs or how they dress. They are just like you and me. We are all connected and we're all one.

Shining Her Light

I have a good friend named Judie who has always been passionate about helping others. She is remarkable because she has never had any expectation that she would get anything back, other than knowing that she is helping.

Thirty years ago, she began volunteering with agencies that serve people with mental illness. As the years went on, she became very familiar with the issues of those suffering with mental illness, and she saw they needed a place where they could go and hang out for friendship and support. Many of these adults are unable to hold a job and are on disability because of their mental illness.

She and her husband decided to take their savings and buy a house in Muskegon, Michigan to create a place where their members could visit during the day. The Lemonade Stand was created in 1998 and is going strong today. It is a drop-in center where everyone is welcome, and members can come for support, friendship, and a meal. They set it up so the members have as much autonomy/ responsibility as possible. Lunch is served every day, and there is a schedule for cleaning and cooking. Because they are a non-profit, Judie arranged to have food donated through a government agency. Judie and her husband not only put up quite a bit of their own money, they have put in thousands of hours over the years in helping to run the "Stand."

People who are mentally ill feel the stigma that comes with this diagnosis, and are often overlooked and ignored by society. Some have families helping them, but many do not. Judie and Larry have created a safe space for them. At their annual Christmas party, she makes sure all members receive Christmas presents. If someone is moving into an apartment, Judie will help them get set up with whatever furnishings they need. I think she is a mother, guardian angel, and good friend rolled into one for many of the members. What if everyone were so blessed to have that kind of support in their lives?

Judie invited me to lunch at the Stand last summer. Once I arrived, I noticed some of the members were in the small kitchen preparing the food, while others hung out in the living room and chatted. Judie and I meandered through the group, and she introduced me to everyone. After a meal of sloppy joes and potato salad, I hung around for a meeting they were having to plan a trip to go dune buggy riding. I was invited to go along, but I wasn't going to be in town that day, so I had to take a rain check. I hope to see them again when I am back visiting in the area.

We are all looking for love, connection, and meaning in our lives. I noticed there was a sense of camaraderie in the group, along with many friendships.

Judie and Larry have created a special place where the members can love and support each other. Where would they be if they were not at the Stand? Many of them would be hanging out somewhere else—very likely isolated and alone.

Judie and Larry are bright lights in their corner of the world, and they have touched hundreds of lives with their selflessness. Judie's work with the Lemonade Stand has always been as a volunteer. She receives no salary or monies for her work. If you have a desire to help Judie and the Lemonade Stand with a donation or by volunteering, it is a registered nonprofit and you can find them on Facebook.

The Power to Affect Change

There was a time when I believed only famous people could make a difference in the world and the rest of us were powerless. Now I know that is a false belief—completely untrue. Like Judie and Larry and the protesters of the peaceful revolution, we all have the power to influence and change things with our thoughts and actions. The Berlin wall fell because thousands of people, through visualization, positive thoughts, and prayer, willed it to be gone. There is no limit to what we can achieve, especially when we do it together.

You and I can be agents of change—we must be agents of change and we start with ourselves. Whatever we want to create in the world, we must first have it in our hearts. Peace? It must be within us. Love? Once it's in our hearts, we can share it with others. In Leipzig, thoughts of peace came first, then peaceful actions. Attracting to themselves what they were thinking about, peace showed up in a way no one dreamed possible: it was all around them, and most amazingly, in their opposition.

Our Reason for Being

We are all here to love and to be loved—that is our true purpose. Every one of us is working on mastering this lesson. This is a journey all of us take on our path to enlightenment. We start by realizing we are special, we are children of God, and we have a fragment of that spirit within us which when manifested, becomes our bright light. **Every time we act with love, we take a step closer to fulfilling our soul's destiny.** Try sending love to everyone you see and keep it in mind. I send love to homeless people, elderly people, babies, children, flowers, cats, trees, and my mom and grandma in heaven, to name a few.

1. Smile at people and open your heart. Don't be afraid to reach out.

2. Reflect on all the kind people who have touched your life and blessed you.

3. Think lovely thoughts. Believe the world can and will get better.

4. Say hello to your neighbors—start a conversation.

5. Choose to be a conduit for peace and love with thoughts, mantras, and prayers. "Peace begins with me." "Peace is everywhere in the world." " I choose peace."

6. We go out in the world knowing the answer to every question is love.

Let peace begin today with us. We can pray, act, and speak words of peace and love every day we're here. We listen for Spirit's messages and trust our intuition to guide us. We can smile at strangers, offer directions to lost tourists, and give someone a quarter for their meter. *We can reach out and be the change we want to see in the world.*

You and I are the peaceful warriors in the next peaceful revolution. We begin our journey together. I will offer you my hand and heart, knowing you will do the same. Let's take our vision and transform, inspire, and create—a new world.

Let peace begin with me.

Mantras

We're all one.

Everything is working in my favor now.

Love solves everything.

I am beautiful and lovable just the way I am.

I deserve to be happy and loved.

I attract great people with great energy into my life.

I give love, respect, and kindness to people and it is returned in kind.

I can create anything I want in life.

I share my life with people I love and who love me.

Every day in every way, I am getting better and better.

Thank you for my strong body and healthy mind.

Peace is everywhere in the world.

Peace begins with me.

Thank you for healthy body and strong mind.

I choose peace.

Thank you for the peace in my life/ in our lives.

Thank you for the wind, rain, heat, and moon. Thank you wind for blowing and stars for shining.

Imagine peace now.

It's a beautiful day to be alive.

Peace be with us.

All my dreams are coming true now.

Peace is everywhere.

Let Peace begin with me.

48050152R00127

Made in the USA
San Bernardino, CA
15 August 2019